Oakton Community College
Morton Grove, Illinois

SYLVIA PLATH

By CAROLINE KING BARNARD

TWAYNE PUBLISHERS

A DIVISION OF G. K. HALL & CO., BOSTON

Library of Congress Cataloging in Publication Data

Barnard, Caroline King.
  Sylvia Plath.

  (Twayne's United States authors series ; TUSAS 309)
  Bibliography: p. 121–28
  Includes index.
  1. Plath, Sylvia—Criticism and interpretation.
PS3566.L27Z58 1978   811'.5'4   78-1862
ISBN 0-8057-7219-7

For
John Reynolds Hall

Contents

About the Author

Caroline K. Barnard did her graduate work in English at Brown University, where her studies emphasized the British novel and modern poetry. In 1973, she received her Ph.D. from Brown. Since 1971, she has been a member of the English faculties of the University of Rhode Island, Fairleigh Dickinson University, and the University of New Orleans.

Preface

Since Sylvia Plath's death in 1963, her writings have attracted increasing numbers of devoted readers. For many high school and college students today, Plath's autobiographical novel *The Bell Jar* is required reading; many readers have been impressed, as well, by her *Ariel* poems. Her published work now includes several short stories, *The Bell Jar*, and over two hundred poems, about two-thirds of which are collected in the volumes *The Colossus, Crossing the Water, Winter Trees*, and *Ariel*. Certainly, Sylvia Plath has achieved in death the recognition she never knew in life.

Plath's work received little critical scrutiny prior to 1964. What attention it did receive consisted principally of brief and largely superficial reviews of *The Colossus and Other Poems* (1960), her first volume of poetry and the only one published during her lifetime. Serious critical interest in her work seems to have begun following the posthumous publication in 1965 of the late *Ariel* poems, her second volume; this interest was sustained by the republication in 1966, under her own name, of *The Bell Jar* (originally published in 1963 under the pseudonym Victoria Lucas) and of the transitional *Crossing the Water* and late *Winter Trees* poems in 1971. Impressed by the technical excellence and the emotional intensity of Plath's late poems, many critics have gone back and reread the earlier writing. Thus, most recent studies examine Plath's work chronologically, agreeing, as I do, on the organicism of her canon.

Sylvia Plath's work invites a chronological reading in terms of the gradual change in her perception of essentially a single subject. Through all of her writing, poetry and fiction, her attention remains fixed on death and disintegration with occasional explorations of their alternatives. There is a definite movement in her work toward greater concreteness of voice and imagery and at the same time toward the blurring of objective-subjective, exterior-interior boundaries, culminating in a group of economical and specific yet hallucinatory, nightmarish poems.

In tracing this development, my study focuses mainly on the speaking voice itself—on the nature of the perception—and on the gradual merging of form with content (insofar as "idea" and "subject" can be said to have been separable from "structure" in the first place). In terms of oral quality, there is a change from a primarily written mode in the early work to a distinctly spoken mode in the late. The trend is toward the effective dramatic poem, with singular focus on a well-characterized, compellingly believable speaker as tone becomes less whimsical and sentimental, more incisive and self-assured.

A chronological examination of Sylvia Plath's writing, then, not only acquaints the reader with the whole work of an important contemporary poet; it also adds valuable dimension to the reader's understanding of the best, late poems. For it is in these poems that Sylvia Plath achieves her finest means of expression and states most successfully the themes which her writings have expressed from the beginning. In my examination of Plath's late poetry—which follows a survey of her earlier work—I hope to articulate my discovery of the special vision to which all of her work attests.

My quotations are from the American editions of *The Bell Jar*, *The Colossus*, *Crossing the Water*, *Winter Trees*, and *Ariel*. (Acknowledgment is made to Harper & Row, Publishers, Inc. for permission to quote from *The Bell Jar, Crossing the Water, Winter Trees* and *Ariel*.) Both the novel and each of the poetry volumes were first published in London; in the case of the poetry, the contents of the English and American versions of each volume differ slightly. I have tried to detail these differences at the beginning of the relevant poetry chapters.

For their advice, counsel, and help in various necessary ways, I wish to thank Robert Scholes, Keith Waldrop, Daniel Marder, Mark Spilka, Richard Harlow, and York and Margaret King. I also offer thanks to the Brown University libraries and to the University of New Orleans Organized Research Fund. I must mention J. B. Wolgamot as well. Finally, kind thanks to Warren French.

CAROLINE K. BARNARD

Chronology

1932   Sylvia Plath born, October 27, in Boston, the first child of Aurelia Schober and Otto Emil Plath.

1936   Family (including younger brother Warren, born 1935) moves to seaside town of Winthrop, Massachusetts.

1940   Father dies.

1942   Family moves inland to Wellesley, Massachusetts.

1942–   Attends public schools in Wellesley. Writes first poems and
1950   short stories.

1950   Receives scholarship to Smith College.

1953   Spends summer in New York as *Mademoiselle* guest editor. Returns home to Wellesley; attempts suicide; is hospitalized.

1954   Returns to Smith; receives scholarship to Harvard summer school.

1955   Graduates from Smith; attends Cambridge University, England, on Fulbright fellowship

1956   June 16, marries Ted Hughes.

1957   Returns with husband to Massachusetts; teaches English for one year at Smith College.

1958   Resides in Boston; writes and attends Robert Lowell's poetry classes at Boston University.

1959   Visits Yaddo; returns to England; resides in London.

1960   April 1, Frieda Rebecca Hughes born. October, publishes *The Colossus and Other Poems*.

1961   Family moves to Devon.

1962   January 17, Nicholas Farrar Hughes born. December, separated from husband, moves with children to London.

1963   January, publishes *The Bell Jar* under the pseudonym, Victoria Lucas. Dies February 11.

1965   *Ariel* published.

1966   *The Bell Jar*.

1971   *Crossing the Water* and *Winter Trees*.

1975   *Letters Home*.

CHAPTER 1

The Life Which Shaped the Work

SYLVIA Plath is a writer whose life has generated unusually keen interest. Such interest is provoked, no doubt, partly by her tragic and untimely death, and partly by the highly personal nature of her writings. She strikes a responsive chord in her readers; many can see in Esther Greenwood, the autobiographical narrator of Plath's very popular novel, *The Bell Jar*, something of themselves. And the intense emotional content of her poems, especially of those included in *Ariel*, evoke awe even in those readers who only partially understand them. Examining Plath's life does, indeed, illuminate one's understanding of her work, for much of the imagery and attitudes and events one finds in Plath's poetry and fiction have their genesis in her life experience. A major biographical objective, then, must be the discovery of the self which is constantly being recreated for us in the literature. For Sylvia Plath, biography is significant ultimately because of her perception of it.

I Seaside Childhood

Throughout her short life, Sylvia Plath loved and was fascinated by the sea. She spent her early years close by the ocean on the Atlantic coast just north of Boston, and this childhood place was marvelous to her, not only inspiring wonder and awe in the child, but also providing the source for much of her later poetic imagery. Indeed, as she writes in one of her letters home, "my ocean-childhood . . . is probably the foundation of my consciousness."[1]

Sylvia Plath was born in Boston, Massachusetts, on October 27, 1932, to Aurelia Schober and Otto Emil Plath. Her father, a professor of biology and German at Boston University, was of German descent, having emigrated from Grabow, in the Polish Corridor, when he was fifteen. Her mother was a first generation American, having been born in Boston of Austrian parents. Their common

Germanic background was indirectly responsible for their meeting; they met in 1929 when Aurelia Schober, working on a master's degree in English and German at Boston University, took a German course taught by Otto Plath. Their common Germanic background was also to become very important to the poetic life of their daughter Sylvia, for it, like the sea, provides a major source for her poetic imagery.

Otto Plath seems to have been guided by the principles of discipline and order; as Mrs. Plath tells us in *Letters Home*, his "Germanic theory that the man should be *der Herr des Hauses* (head of the house) persisted" (*L,* 13). On the day Sylvia was born, as Mrs. Plath relates, he announced that " 'I hope for one more thing in life—a son, two and a half years from now.' Warren was born April 27, 1935, only two hours off schedule, and Otto was greeted by his colleagues as 'the man who gets what he wants when he wants it' " (*L,* 12). As his young family grew, Otto Plath's academic career flourished; shortly after Sylvia's birth he published the book *Bumblebees and Their Ways,* and for the first four years of Sylvia's life he devoted much time to scholarly writing, excluding nearly any possibility for social life. As part of his interest in entomology, however, he did keep bees, an activity later pursued by his daughter. A number of her poems, indeed, commemorate this common interest of father and daughter; these are the so-called "Bee poems" of the late volume *Ariel* ("The Bee Meeting," "The Arrival of the Bee Box," "Stings," "The Swarm," and "Wintering") and the *Colossus* poem "The Beekeeper's Daughter."

In 1936, the family moved to the ocean, to Winthrop, Massachusetts. Otto's health had begun to fail, but, having diagnosed his illness as lung cancer, he refused to see a doctor. He drove himself to continue teaching and his health deteriorated further. But if this was a difficult time at home for Sylvia, it was also a wondrous time for her near the sea. Because her father required much rest and quiet, Sylvia spent many hours outdoors at the beach, exploring by herself, or playing with her brother or with neighbors, or visiting with her maternal grandparents who lived nearby on the ocean at Point Shirley. Later in her life, Plath was to recall these early seaside years in the settings of many of her poems ("Point Shirley," "Suicide Off Egg Rock," and "The Hermit at Outermost House," for example), and to write about them specifically in the autobiographical sketch "Ocean 1212-W" (her grandparents' telephone number), re-creating the sights and sounds and smells of the oceanside which made such an indelible impression on both her early and her later life.

On the day before Sylvia's tenth birthday, in 1942, the family moved away from the sea. Two years earlier, Otto Plath had died, a victim of diabetes mellitus. Since he had refused medical attention for three years after becoming ill, his malady was correctly diagnosed too late to save his life. Aurelia Plath had found it necessary to return to work to support her family, and, despite health problems of her own, had been teaching nearby. Sylvia meanwhile had developed sinusitis, and Warren bronchitis. So, in the summer of 1942, when Aurelia Plath was offered the job of designing and teaching a course in medical secretarial procedures at Boston University, the whole family—Sylvia, Warren, and Aurelia Plath, and Sylvia's maternal grandparents, the Schobers—left the ocean and moved to Wellesley, Massachusetts. There, while Sylvia went to school and her mother went to work, her grandfather found employment nearby and her grandmother took charge of the housework.

II *The Wellesley Years: Developing Habits*

Sylvia Plath's eight years in Wellesley marked a time of growth and development, a time when writing and academic achievement became increasingly important to her. She was a bright child, an A student; when she moved to Wellesley, she was initially placed in the sixth grade, two years ahead of her chronological peers (her mother had her moved back to fifth). She continued her piano lessons, begun in Winthrop when she was seven, and began to study the viola. She joined the Girl Scouts, and attended a Girl Scout camp on Cape Cod for several summers. During the years when she attended the Wellesley public grammar, junior high, and senior high schools, her precocity, so apparent throughout her later career, became increasingly evident. As her mother observed in *Letters Home*, "it was in junior high that she developed work habits and skill in her favorite fields of endeavor, art and writing, winning prizes from the 'scholastic awards' competitions each year" (*L*, 31). Finally, just before leaving for college, Sylvia was awarded a new and long-sought prize; after numerous rejections, her first story,

"And Summer Will Not Come Again," was published in the August, 1950, issue of *Seventeen*. And on the following November, the same magazine published her poem "Ode on a Bitten Plum."

During her Wellesley years, Sylvia Plath's activities and accomplishments reveal her as a bright, happy, and successful person. Yet her very success bred problems which were to threaten her equilibrium later in her life and which were to manifest themselves in her writing. Feeling keenly divided by the apparently incompatible social and intellectual roles she was asked to play, she developed for herself a social mask, establishing the duality of self so evident in the speakers of *The Bell Jar* and her later poetry. As her mother notes, "Sylvia was conscious of the prejudice boys built up among themselves about 'brainy' girls. By the time she was a senior in high school, she had learned to hide behind a façade of light-hearted wit when in a mixed group," so that her greatest joy was not being believed by a date to whom she laughingly revealed that she was a straight A student (*L*, 38). At the same time, recalls her mother, Sylvia's writing began to reveal "an examination and analysis of the darker recesses of self." This direction, according to Mrs. Plath, is explained by the fact of Sylvia's discovering that "problem" literature sold better than "exuberant, joyous outbursts" (*L*, 35, 36). But we may question that assessment in light of the poet's later work.

Another problem bred by—and also no doubt responsible for—Sylvia Plath's accomplishments during this period was the impossibly high goals she set for herself. "I want, I think, to be omniscient," she wrote. "I think I would like to call myself 'the girl who wanted to be God.' Yet if I were not in this body, where would I be—perhaps I am *destined* to be classified and qualified. But, oh, I cry out against it" (*L*, 40). Certainly many idealistic, intelligent seventeen-year-olds have expressed similar sentiments. But in Sylvia Plath they signal the perfectionist attitude which drove her to succeed at the same time that it insured failure, breeding a kind of destructive energy which was to become increasingly evident in her writing. As she observes, "I have erected in my mind an image of myself—idealistic and beautiful. Is not that image, free from blemish, the true self—the true perfection? Am I wrong when this image insinuates itself between me and the merciless mirror? . . . Never, never will I reach the perfection I long for with all my soul—my paintings, my poems, my stories—all poor, poor reflections" (*L*, 40).

III   *Smith College: Brilliance and Breakdown*

Although her personal and professional accomplishments had become a source not only of satisfaction but also of frustration, Sylvia Plath continued her well-established habit of award and prize winning. In September, 1950, she entered Smith College, the recipient of financial aid from the Nielson scholarship, the Smith Club of Wellesley, and the Olive Higgins Prouty Fund. Delighted and inspired by the challenging and fertile atmosphere she found there, she thrived both socially and academically. She continued, however, to have difficulty integrating the two; she needed, she said, to "unobtrusively do well in all my courses" (*L*, 48). But if Plath's self-image continued to fall short of the perfection she desired, she managed to affect a "nonbrainy" appearance while appearing vibrant and confident to others. One of her roommates, Nancy Hunter Steiner, describes Sylvia's "clothes and manner" as "deliberately cultivated to disguise any distinction. . . . Sylvia was a remarkably attractive young woman. She was impressively tall, almost statuesque, and she carried the height with an air of easy assurance. . . . The face was angular and its features strong."[2]

Plath continued to write poems and stories and to send them off to publishers. Aurelia Plath at this time became her daughter's part-time agent and typist, providing for her the encouragement and clerical assistance which she had previously offered her husband. Such support at once lent impetus to Sylvia's career and increased her anxiety, for she now felt driven to succeed in order to reward not only herself but also her mother. "I hope," she wrote to her mother, "I can continue to lay more laurels at your feet" (*L*, 94). But she sensed, as well, the threat posed by her mother's efforts. Writing to her brother, Sylvia observed that their mother "is an abnormally altruistic person, and I have realized lately that we have to fight against her selflessness as we would fight against a deadly disease." But, she continues, "After extracting her life blood and care for 20 years, we should start bringing in big dividends of joy for her" (*L*, 112, 113).

Whatever the source of her inspiration, however, Plath continued to fare brilliantly in her writing and in her schoolwork. She enjoyed increasing success with publication and with publication prizes, especially in *Mademoiselle*, *Seventeen*, and *Harper's* magazines. She became an honors student. Any hint of professional, social, or academic rejection spelled failure to her, but generally she seemed able to cope, realizing the therapeutic value of hope and humor. One should, she observed, *"never . . .* commit suicide, because something unexpected always happens." And, "in spite of everything, I still have my good old sense of humor" (*L,* 58, 90).

Among her most cherished prizes was the *Mademoiselle* guest editorship she was awarded for the summer of 1953. In June, along with nineteen other college women, Plath went to New York to produce the annual *Mademoiselle* college issue. She was assigned to be managing editor (a disappointment, since she had hoped to be fiction editor), and her duties included interviews with Elizabeth Bowen and with several poets (among them Richard Wilbur and George Steiner) for her "Poets on Campus" feature. New York itself, along with the social activities planned for her group, offered a new, exciting, and bewildering experience. She felt at once stimulated and disoriented, so that sometimes, she confessed in a letter to her brother, "I can't think logically about who I am or where I am going. I have been very ecstatic, horribly depressed, shocked, elated, enlightened, and enervated" (*L,* 117). At the end of June she left for Boston exhausted and depressed. "I will let you know what train my coffin will come in on" (*L,* 120), she wrote her brother.

Plath's experience in New York, and the events of the following six months, are compellingly portrayed in her autobiographical novel, *The Bell Jar.* Returning home, she learned of her rejection from a fiction-writing class at Harvard summer school; her depression and sense of failure intensified. She tried to learn shorthand and to read, but could not concentrate. Her mother sought psychiatric help, which resulted in a series of bungled shock treatments. Finally, in August, Sylvia left a note saying that she had gone for a walk, crawled under her house, and swallowed a large number of sleeping pills. Three days later she was discovered there and rushed to a hospital. Unable to cope and, as she believed, unable to live up to others' expectations of her, she had attempted suicide. Her act, she told her mother, was "my last act of love" (*L,* 125–26).

She recovered in a private hospital suggested by her faithful benefactress, Olive Higgins Prouty. Her doctor understood her difficulty; as Mrs. Prouty wrote to Sylvia's mother, "Dr. B. suggested that she is a perfectionist, which accounts for her self-depreciation if she falls short of perfection in anything she does" (*L,* 128).

By December, Sylvia felt emotionally and physically strong enough to plan a return to Smith for the second semester—as she observes in *The Bell Jar*, "patched, retreaded and approved for the road."[3]

Plath's last three semesters were marked by the same activity and success that had marked her first three college years. She wrote and published more poems and stories, attended Harvard summer school on scholarship, and received several new awards and prizes. Her English honors thesis, on the literary treatment of the double, provides an interesting gloss to her later poetic imagery and personae. Her reading, she reported, included "fascinating stuff about the ego as symbolized in reflections (mirror and water), shadows, twins—dividing off and becoming an enemy, or omen of death, or a warning conscience, or a means by which one denies the power of death (e.g., by creating the idea of the soul as the deathless double of the mortal body)" (*L*, 146).

In June, 1955, Sylvia Plath graduated *summa cum laude* from Smith and—having received a Fulbright fellowship to Cambridge University—prepared to depart for England.

IV *Branching Out: Career and Marriage*

The seven years which followed marked a period of great activity and promise in Sylvia Plath's life. It was a time of awakening and maturation, a time filled with experiences both new and momentous to the course of her personal and professional development. In these years, Plath traveled widely; for a time, she wrote more prolifically than ever before; and she married.

In England, Plath continued to enjoy the same academic achievement and success which had marked her previous school years. Her two years as a Fulbright scholar at Newnham College, Cambridge, were joyful and exciting ones. In addition to writing regularly and reading for her examination, she joined the university's Dramatic Society, modeled and wrote for the Cambridge newspaper *Varsity*, vacationed in France, and maintained an active social life. In March, 1956, Sylvia met the British poet Ted Hughes, and on the following June 16, Bloomsday, they were married. They traveled to Spain for the summer, renting rooms in Benidorm, a small Mediterranean village. There, with her new husband, Plath began to establish an important daily routine to allow her sufficient time for the writing which had become for her a daily necessity.

Returning to Cambridge in the fall, the Hugheses rented an apartment near Grantchester. Sylvia resumed her studies at Newnham, while Ted got a job teaching at a boys' school. As important as her own writing was to her, Sylvia now apparently initiated the practice of professional deference to her husband. Like her mother before her, Sylvia became typist and agent for someone she loved, devoting much time and energy distributing Ted's poems to potential publishers. About the 1957 publication of his first volume of poetry, she wrote. "I am more happy than if it was my book published! I have worked so closely on these poems of Ted's and typed them so many countless times through revision after revision that I feel ecstatic about it all. I am so happy *his* book is accepted *first*. . . . I can rejoice, then, much more, knowing Ted is ahead of me" (*L*, 297).

Nonetheless, Plath did find time in that year for her own work as well, and, in addition to supporting her husband's budding career, published a number of stories and poems in such journals as *Poetry*, *Atlantic*, and the Cambridge magazine *Granta*. In May, she took her examinations, in which she excelled. By this time, the Hugheses were ready to move on. Ted had felt increasingly burdened by his teaching duties, which deprived him of the time and energy he preferred to spend in writing. Sylvia, who was eager to return to America, therefore accepted a job teaching freshman English at Smith College; and the Hugheses sailed for New York in June, 1957.

Back in Northampton, Sylvia experienced the same frustration as Ted had known the previous year; her teaching duties, she found, left too little time for her writing. Therefore, when the school year ended, the Hugheses moved to Boston. They rented a small Beacon Hill apartment, planning to support themselves by their writing as best they could. To supplement their income, Sylvia held several part-time jobs; she worked in a hospital and in a psychiatrist's office, experiences which provided material for her stories "The Daughters of Blossom Street" and "Johnny Panic and the Bible of Dreams." She also attended Robert Lowell's poetry class at Boston University, where she came to know several other young poets, among them Anne Sexton and George Starbuck.

After one year in Boston, however, in the summer of 1959, the Hugheses planned a return to England. Ted had been awarded a Guggenheim grant for the next year's writing; furthermore, he wished for the child which he and Sylvia now planned to be born in his native land. Before leaving the United States, however, Sylvia and Ted toured the country, traveling first to California to visit Sylvia's paternal aunt, Frieda, then spending the months of September and October in the writers' colony at Yaddo, New York, where Sylvia wrote many of her *Colossus* poems. After a Thanksgiving spent in Wellesley with Sylvia's mother, the Hugheses departed for London.

In December, 1959, Sylvia and Ted settled into a small flat near Regent's Park. They spent the winter writing, reading, and developing new friendships; early in 1960, Sylvia signed a contract with William Heinemann for her first poetry volume, *The Colossus and Other Poems*, and Ted's second volume was published. On April 1, 1960, Frieda Rebecca Hughes was born. Although the birth of her first child was wonderful to her, Plath found the following year increasingly difficult. Her duties as mother, wife, and secretary left her little time to write, and the submissive conjugal role which she accepted contributed to a growing sense of personal unfulfillment.

To most of their new friends, Sylvia was merely Ted's wife. As one of these friends, A. Alvarez, later observed, "Sylvia seemed effaced, the poet taking a back seat to the young mother and housewife."[4] Although Plath cultivated this identity, she also disliked it. She longed for friends of her own; "I have so missed a good American girl friend!" she wrote (*L*, 383). Ted's career flourished. He maintained a study away from their small apartment, at the homes of various neighbors and friends, where he could write regularly; he gave readings, published prolifically, won many prizes, and achieved increasing recognition. Sylvia, meanwhile, commented: "I really hunger for a study of my own out of hearing of the nursery where I could be alone with my thoughts for a few hours a day" (*L*, 392). She was able to write little, and *The Colossus and Other Poems*, published in November, won no prize and received little publicity. To add to her troubles, Plath's health was poor. In the winter, her sinusitis recurred and she developed appendicitis. Pregnant for the second time, she miscarried in early February, 1961; and she had an appendectomy later in the month.

The spring, however, brought a renewal of personal and professional promise. Plath at last located a study of her own and resumed her writing, working on, among other things, her novel *The Bell Jar*. She signed a long-term contract for her poems with the

New Yorker in March, and in May she received the good news that Alfred A. Knopf planned to publish *The Colossus* in America. She became pregnant again, and she and her husband decided to move to more spacious quarters in the country, where the children could grow and where each parent could have a private study. In September, 1961, they bought an ancient, thatch-roofed manor house in Devon, an hour's drive from the sea.

V   *The Final Years*

For a time, life in their new country home proved fruitful and rewarding. The Hugheses established a writing schedule, enabling Sylvia to write in the morning while Ted wrote in the afternoon. Plath edited an anthology of American poets for the *Critical Quarterly*, and in November was awarded a year's Saxton grant to write poetry. Nicholas Farrar Hughes was born in January, 1962. In May, *The Colossus* was published in America, and in June, Plath's voice play, "Three Women," was accepted for the BBC Third Programme. In June, as well, Sylvia began keeping bees.

But by summer, new trouble appeared. The Hughes marriage had begun to fail. As Sylvia's mother observed during a June, 1962, visit to Devon, "the marriage was seriously troubled, and there was a great deal of anxiety in the air. Ted had been seeing someone else" (*L*, 458). By summer's end, Ted had moved to London, and Sylvia had initiated arrangements for an agreement of legal separation, to be followed by divorce.

Alone in Devon with her two children, Plath was alternately depressed and hopeful, but always busy. She learned to ride (on her horse named Ariel), and looked forward to adjusting to her new freedom. She wrote voluminously, between four and eight every morning, composing, as she said, "a poem a day before breakfast. . . . Terrific stuff, as if domesticity had choked me" (*L*, 466). Her novel, *The Bell Jar*, was accepted for publication; she began work on a second novel and anticipated writing a third. In October, she observed that "I am writing the best poems of my life" (*L*, 468). By December, she had completed thirty poems, which she saw as her second volume.

Ill health, however, plagued her throughout the fall; she suffered recurrent trouble with the flu and with high fever. And she grew to feel increasingly isolated in Devon: "Stuck down here, as into a sack, I fight for air and freedom and the culture and libraries of a city" (*L*, 465). The bell jar had begun to descend again. She planned, therefore, a restorative vacation in Ireland near the sea later in the winter, to be followed by a move to London where she could continue her work in a livelier cultural environment.

"I am fighting now," Plath observed in October, "against hard odds and alone" (*L*, 469). Difficult though it was, she continued the fight. Abandoning her plans for Ireland, she moved in December to London. The flat she found there was near the place she had shared with her husband a year and a half earlier, but it held great promise for her. It was in W. B. Yeats's former house, and she considered it an ideal place for personal rejuvenation and continued professional success. Although her health was not completely restored and the London winter was unusually cold, Plath maintained the pace she had established for herself, decorating her new apartment and working on her *Ariel* poems in the early morning. She began to gain growing professional recognition in her own right; she made several BBC broadcasts and planned to do more, had new poems accepted for publication, did some reviewing, and planned several poetry readings.

She seemed, for a time, to be winning her fight. "The next five years of my life look heavenly," she wrote in December 1962— "school terms in London, summer in Devon" (*L*, 490). However, the odds against her must have seemed too great. On the morning of February 11, 1963, she ended her life.

CHAPTER 2

The Bell Jar

D URING 1961 and early 1962, a period both of great personal difficulty and great creative productivity, Sylvia Plath worked on her autobiographical novel, *The Bell Jar*. Even as she wrote it, Plath must have sensed the shock its appearance in print might cause those people whom she had adapted to her fictional use as well as the discomfort its revelations, now made public, might bring to her, for she was at once pleased by its acceptance for publication and reticent to accept responsibility for its authorship. In her frequent letters to her mother, she made no mention of her work; in a letter to her brother, she noted its acceptance, but cautioned: "This is a secret; it is a pot-boiler and no one must read it!" (*L*, 472). In January, 1963, the novel was published pseudonymously under the name "Victoria Lucas."

Recording a period of confusion, disintegration, and renewal in the life of its protagonist and narrator, Esther Greenwood, *The Bell Jar* draws its materials primarily from the time of Sylvia Plath's *Mademoiselle* guest editorship in the summer of 1953, through her subsequent breakdown and attempted suicide, to the time when, sufficiently rehabilitated, she returned to college. The novel no doubt represents an attempt on its author's part to place these turbulent months in mature perspective, for it records Esther Greenwood's struggle to connect knowledge with experience, past with present and future, and desire with reality.

I *Disintegration*

The subject of Sylvia Plath's English honors thesis, on which she worked after returning to college in 1954, was the literary treatment of the double. In *The Bell Jar*, Plath not only creates a similar scholarly interest for Esther Greenwood; she also provides fictional realization of the device. Elly Higginbottom is Esther Greenwood's other self, the embodiment of her fantasy. Esther's dilemma, her "split personality"[1] as she calls it, is dramatized in the novel's opening chapter by her inability to decide between two potential "best friends." Vacillating between the innocent, wholesome Betsy and the urbane, sexy Doreen, she finds herself unable to form a complete identification with either one, since she herself is divided, in a similar way, between conditioning and desire. To express that inner division, Esther Greenwood creates Elly Higginbottom.

Elly Higginbottom tries, like Doreen, to be worldly and sexually sophisticated. Whatever Esther Greenwood is, Elly represents the Other, and, at the same time that Elly embodies Esther's wish fulfillment, her otherness is complete. Esther is insecure; Elly is supremely self-confident. Esther lives in Boston, a place where she feels constrained by people like her mother and Mrs. Willard to be sexually proper and conventional; Elly comes from Chicago, a place safely distant, "the sort of place where unconventional, mixed-up people would come from" (*B*, 148). Confesses Esther as she assumes her Elly guise: "I didn't want anything I said or did that night to be associated with me and my real name" (*B*, 13). Thus, Elly can attempt to discard the restraining shyness and social insecurity of Esther and seek pick-up dates with Frankie or the Boston sailor. Esther is a scholarship student from a "big eastern women's college" who reads books and writes "long papers on the twins in James Joyce" (*B*, 148) and is dreadfully afraid of marriage; Elly, who is no student, dreams of marrying a "virile but tender garage mechanic and hav[ing] a big cowy family" (*B*, 149). Esther feels smothered by the expectations of family and friends; Elly is an orphan.

It is appropriate for Elly to have neither family nor roots, for she represents escape from all of the pressures which are the source of Esther's present confusion. In so doing, she brings that confusion into sharper relief. Esther is an unwilling captive of her background and conditioning; external familial and social pressures war with her natural instincts, and her level of self-confidence is far too low for those instincts to assert themselves sufficiently. Her naive expectations of sex and marriage, for example, have been thoroughly conditioned by her mother and by others: to be acceptable as a wife she must remain a virgin, and after marriage she must assume a submissive domestic role. Instinctively she rebels against these notions, partly because she naturally senses their limitations, and partly because she discovers that men are not bound by similar premarital rules. The confusion thereby produced is extreme. For nineteen-year-old Esther, "pureness [is] the great issue" (*B*, 90). Because she does not want "infinite security and to be the place an arrow shoots off from" (*B*, 92), as advocated by Buddy Willard and his mother, she decides that she must never marry. And because she now sees "the world divided into people who had slept with somebody and people who hadn't," she resolves to cross "the boundary line" (*B*, 90). Yet her conditioning remains a powerful influence; she can be comfortable with neither alternative.

Indeed, Esther finds it impossible to pursue either alternative in even a remotely satisfying way. "I wondered," she muses, "why I couldn't go the whole way doing what I should any more. This made me sad and tired. Then I wondered why I couldn't go the whole way doing what I shouldn't, . . . and this made me even sadder and more tired" (*B*, 32). This is the tiredness of depression which Esther feels, a depression produced by the immobility which baffles and frustrates her. Esther is indeed trapped within the stifling confines of the bell jar.

Unable to establish and nurture a self-identity which will afford her some measure of security, Esther is reduced to deriving her identity from the expectations of others. She acts. For Doreen, she must be worldly and blasé; for Buddy Willard, she must be pure and virginal; for Jay Cee, she must be intelligent and ambitious; for Mrs. Willard, she must be domestic and submissive. For her mother, she must be the good daughter, appropriately grateful, successful, and innocent. And above all, she must maintain at any cost a proper appearance of health and sanity, not, as her mother puts it, "like that," like "those awful dead people at that hospital" (*B*, 163). The more Esther acts in these ways, the more she loses touch with her self. The result is further loss of confidence and growing disorientation.

Another result of her role-playing is that Esther feels placed in an increasingly defensive position, for in responding to the expectations of others, she allows herself to be constantly acted upon. She comes, therefore, to see her environment as increasingly hostile and threatening. Things accost her. On a skiing trip with Buddy, the rope tow is a "rough, bruising snake of a rope that slithered through [my fingers] " (*B*, 106). People menace her. Elly-Esther is terrified by the "brown figure in sensible flat brown shoes" (*B*, 150) whose appearance on the Boston Common abruptly ends her conversation with the sailor; in the presence of this ominous Mrs. Willard–Mrs. Greenwood person, Esther feels stricken with fear and guilt about her present behavior. She also experiences a sudden, sharp insight: "I thought what an awful woman that lady in the brown suit had been, and how she . . . was responsible for my taking the wrong turn here and the wrong path there and for everything bad that happened after that" (*B*, 151). Men especially threaten her; their reality always fails her expectation. The woman-hating Marco actually attacks her. From her experience with Buddy Willard, she knows that as "flawless" as men may seem "off in the distance," they would not "do at all" when they "moved closer" (*B*, 92). Marriage, then, is impossible for Esther, since she knows that any man, even the handsome Constantin, would require that his wife become a domestic drudge, like Mrs. Willard's kitchen mat. Sex terrifies her; Esther's description of Buddy's penis is particularly devastating and dehumanizing: "The only thing I could think of was turkey neck and turkey gizzards" (*B*, 75).

It is this frame of mind which the novel's Rosenberg motif illuminates. The summer Esther Greenwood goes to New York is also, as *The Bell Jar's* opening lines reveal, "the summer they electrocuted the Rosenbergs" (*B*, 1). Esther observes: "It had nothing to do with me, but I couldn't help wondering what it would be like, being burned alive all along your nerves" (*B*, 1). Despite the disclaimer, the Rosenbergs' experience comes to have a great deal to do with Esther. By the time she becomes Dr. Gordon's patient, her confusion is far advanced; virtually incapable of action, she has become the helpless object of the acts of others. The clumsily applied shock treatment represents the epitome of such acts, and significantly, it comes to serve as the symbol of Esther's paranoia and the total collapse of her perspective. The Rosenbergs, possibly innocent, but helpless before the judgment of their accusers, have been put to death by electrocution. Esther instinctively equates their experience with her own; like the Rosenbergs, she feels powerless and victimized, threatened and judged by everyone and everything. Thus, as her own experience with electric shock commences, Esther wonders "what terrible thing it was that I had done" (*B*, 161).

II   The Bell Jar

Placed in such a precarious emotional position by her insecurity and disorientation, the embattled Esther finds it more and more difficult to connect inner with outer reality. She is caught in a vicious round of destructive activity, for, as her behavior has indicated, her very efforts at coping with her world also reinforce her isolation. Her voice expresses the dilemma. Esther's tone, especially up to the time of her recovery under Dr. Nolan's guidance, is similar to the tone of such late poems as "Lady Lazarus" and "The Applicant": carefully postured, mocking, caustic, defensively nonchalant. It is the voice which Esther feels encouraged by Doreen's influence to develop: "wise and cynical as all hell" (B, 9). Esther's wit is brilliant, and her humorous observations are incisive. Such a voice can protect, but it can also protect too well, building an impregnable barrier between its speaker and the world, between the self and other people.

This condition is realized in the novel's dominant image; Esther feels as though she is "being stuffed farther and farther into a black, airless sack with no way out" (B, 144). She is increasingly unable to deal with her environment, progressively helpless to "steer anything, not even myself," powerless to "get myself to react" (B, 3). The glass walls of the bell jar permit only a tantalizing, often distorted visual contact between inside and outside; all other forms of mutual communication are impossible. And the interior environment not only isolates; it stifles. Esther observes: "The air of the bell jar wadded round me and I couldn't stir" (B, 210).

Total withdrawal becomes Esther's only course of action. "To the person in the bell jar . . . the world itself is the bad dream" (B, 267), she concludes, and escape from that present dream with its impossible demands and pressures can be achieved only by return to an earlier, simpler time. "I was only purely happy," she observes, "until I was nine years old" (B, 82): what she seeks, then, is the singleness, the simplicity, and the purity of infancy.

The actions which Esther takes to achieve this end involve a kind of ritual purgation, a means by which she can free herself of uncleanliness or confusion or guilt. To restore herself to a state of simple purity, she must destroy or dissolve all evidence of the present "bad dream." It is this kind of action which Sylvia Plath employs also in the imagery of many of her last poems; release from the oppression of the speaker's present condition is often expressed in terms of death, purification, and rebirth. Similarly, Esther Greenwood, having returned from an evening of being Elly with Doreen and Lenny, seeks to rid herself of the whole dirty, oppressive experience through the rebirth of a sort of baptism:

I said to myself: "Doreen is dissolving, Lenny Shepherd is dissolving, Frankie is dissolving, New York is dissolving, they are all dissolving away and none of them matter any more. I don't know them, I have never known them and I am very pure. All that liquor and those sticky kisses I saw and the dirt that settled on my skin on the way back is turning to something pure."

The longer I lay there in the clear hot water the purer I felt, and when I stepped out at last and wrapped myself in one of the big, soft white hotel bath towels I felt pure and sweet as a new baby. (*B*, 22)

The bath, in this case, achieves the required retrogression, restoring Esther's spirit without doing violence to her body. As her sense of oppression intensifies, however, so does her need for escape, rendering her ever more careless of physical consequences. Buddy Willard's proposal of marriage places Esther in a particularly critical position, especially since her refusal expresses a rebellion she is not equipped to handle. Skiing with Buddy shortly thereafter, then, she again seeks to rid herself of her present world with its intolerable pressures and demands; this time her need is so great that even the death of her physical body is of no consequence: "the thought that I might kill myself formed in my mind coolly as a tree or a flower" (*B*, 107). An inexperienced skier, she takes off down the hill: "I thought, 'this is what it is to be happy.' I plummeted down past the zigzaggers, the students, the experts, through year after year of doubleness and smiles and compromise, into my own past. People and trees receded on either hand like the dark sides of a tunnel as I hurtled on to the still, bright point at the end of it, the pebble at the bottom of the well, the white sweet baby cradled in its mother's belly" (*B*, 108).

From here, there is only a small step to Esther's actual suicide attempt, for that act represents for her a total withdrawal to the "pure" and "sweet" condition of infancy. The location she chooses is a dark hole beneath her house, a "secret, earth-bottomed crevice" leading from the cellar, which is lit only by "a dim, undersea light." After some effort, Esther crawls into the hole, "crouch[ing] at the mouth of the darkness," and covers the entrance with a log. The earth inside her womb-like retreat is "friendly"; the dark feels "thick as velvet"; the cobwebs are soft; she curls up and takes her sleeping pills (B, 190–91).

III *Recovery and Prognosis*

From this experience, Esther does achieve a sort of rebirth, though perhaps not precisely the variety she had expected. Her suicide attempt fails, and she is hospitalized. Yet, in her total collapse, she has reached a kind of infancy, from which she can grow. Depressed beyond the point of caring about "the doubleness and smiles and compromise," and encouraged by the sensitive Dr. Nolan to rediscover herself on her own terms, Esther slowly constructs for herself a new and better integrated personality.

She learns to free herself from the tyranny of others' expectations. Helpless to act even defensively during the days immediately following her suicide attempt, she has no choice but to appear exactly as she is. Her legs may look "disgusting and ugly" when Buddy Willard comes to visit, but she makes no move to hide them. " 'That's me,' " she thinks. " 'That's what I am' " (B, 195). When a group of medical students passing her bed greet her with the customary "How are you feeling?" she responds not with the expected "Fine" but with a truthful "I feel lousy" (B, 200). Once she is able to reveal her true self in this rudimentary way, Esther develops new confidence and perspective. In the presence of her hospital visitors, she identifies the tyranny which has held her captive, and she grows to hate these visits, since she knows that the visitors measure her "fat and stringy hair against what I had been and what they wanted me to be" (B, 228). She now sees that such an attitude has motivated even the apparently beneficent interest of people like Jay Cee and the famous career-oriented woman poet at her college: "they all wanted to adopt me in some way, and, for the price of their care and influence, have me resemble them" (B, 248). Slowly Esther grows to understand the futility of building her identity on the expectations of people like these.

Perhaps the visitor most threatening to Esther's new perspective is her mother. Of all the forces which have kept Esther divided against herself, her mother has been the most powerful, looming up as she did that day on the Boston Common to assert her influence. Pious self-abnegation has been one of the mother's tools, and she attempts to use it still; during one of her visits, "my mother told me I should be grateful. She said I had used up almost all her money" (*B*, 209). Guilt keeps the daughter under control, and Esther, while seeing herself manipulated in this way, nevertheless feels the bell jar descending around her once again. On other occasions, however, Esther challenges her mother's influence more successfully. Of all her visitors, Esther observes, "my mother was the worst. She never scolded me, but kept begging me, with a sorrowful face, to tell her what she had done wrong" (*B*, 228). Following one of these sessions she dares to reveal to Dr. Nolan that she hates her mother—and then waits "for the blow to fall." Marvelously, however, Dr. Nolan replies only that " 'I suppose you do' " (*B*, 229). With such support, Esther grows able to accept and deal with her rebellion. She recalls a recent visit from her mother, her face "a pale, reproachful moon." "A daughter in an asylum! I had done that to her" had been the mother's implied message. And "with her sweet, martyr's smile," she had said: " 'We'll take up where we left off, Esther. . . . We'll act as if this were a bad dream' " (*B*, 267). But Esther now knows that she must do nothing of the kind.

Indeed, Esther achieves sufficient perspective to see that her struggle against the tyranny of custom and expectation is not hers alone, but is generally characteristic of the human condition. Her hospital environment is little different from the college environment which she has left and to which she will return. Like her and her hospital friends, her college friends, "too, sat under bell jars of a sort" (*B*, 268). Further, her new perspective allows her to deal with the "bad dream" from which her mother wishes her to seek escape. "Remember[ing] everything," she can now shun the idea that "forgetfulness, like a kind of snow, should numb and cover" the particulars of that nightmare. For "they were part of me. They were my landscape" (*B*, 267). The bell jar has been raised; it now hangs, "suspended, a few feet above my head. I was open to the circulating air" (*B*, 242).

Several other events herald Esther's emergence from the stifling confines of the bell jar. For the first time since the opening of her narrative, she laughs. In a conversation with Buddy Willard concerning the suicide of their friend Joan, Esther, confident in her own evaluation of the situation and accurate in her assessment of Buddy's confusion, "burst out laughing" (*B*, 270). To be sure, Esther's observations throughout the course of her narrative have not been without humor, but this laugh is different. This is not, like the others, an inward-directed, self-conscious quip or a sardonic gibe; it is the outward-directed, spontaneous response of a person secure enough to have no need of sarcasm. And that laugh, as it signals Esther's new freedom from the tyranny of her old self, provides a new perspective for the reader as well; the barriers between Esther and the world are removed not only for Esther, but also for her audience.

Joan's death affords Esther another opportunity to exercise her new perspective. During the conversation in which Esther laughs, Buddy is concerned that he, somehow, is responsible for the suicide attempts of Joan and Esther, both of whom he had dated. Esther, having already overcome, with Dr. Nolan's help, the fear of her own culpability, now assumes the role of healer as she allays Buddy's apprehensions. Even more important for Esther, however, is the symbolic significance of Joan's death. "I wondered," she muses at Joan's funeral, "what I thought I was burying" (B, 273). Like the old Esther, Joan has been tyrannized by the brown Boston Common mother figure, yet Joan has been unable to identify the source of her oppression. Unlike Esther, Joan has been eager for Buddy to bring his mother to visit at the hospital. Thus, Esther now knows that Joan is a reminder "of what I had been, and what I had been through" (B, 246). Joan's burial, then, signifies an aspect of Esther's new freedom, for what Esther buries at Joan's funeral is a part of her old, captive self.

Another symbol of Esther's new freedom is her diaphragm. As she points out, its acquisition frees her from the fear of unwanted pregnancy with its several undesirable consequences. She is no longer a sexual victim; even though her fear of marriage persists, she may now control her own fate. And the liberation afforded by this new control permits Esther to come to terms with her sexual identity. Able now to put aside the blandishments of her mother and Mrs. Willard, Esther is free to shed the virginity which has been such an intolerable psychological burden to her old self. She thus will be able to resolve the ambivalence which has so destructively divided her; the division of character represented by the former, oppressed Esther and her wish-fulfilling Elly Higginbottom is no longer necessary. Significantly, as Esther narrates the particulars of her tryst with Irwin, on whom she practices her "new, normal personality" (B, 254), she fails to mention the name by which Irwin called her. Surely she is no longer Elly, even though this experience is a sexual one. In leaving her narrator nameless, Plath represents the narrator's new wholeness, for she is not now the old Esther, either. She is truly, as she observes, "my own woman" (*B*, 251).

Thus renewed, Esther awaits her expected dismissal from the hospital. She has been, as she puts it, "born twice—patched, re-treaded and approved for the road" (*B*, 275). The reader may safely assume that Esther's recovery is complete. Her prognosis seems good; the "new, normal personality" with which she now meets the world may well be sufficiently strong to resist future breakdown. Indeed, at the time when she actually tells this story, Esther is someone's wife and the mother of a baby; she is, she says, "all right" (*B*, 4), and she uses some of the free gifts from her chaotic summer in New York as toys for her child.

There is, however, a note of warning also sounded at the novel's close. A retreaded tire, surely, can come apart more readily than a new one. Further, Esther the narrator-character asks: "How did I know that someday—at college, in Europe, somewhere, any-where—the bell jar, with its stifling distortions, wouldn't descend again?" (*B*, 271) Perhaps this question offers further corroboration of Esther's new, realistic self. On the other hand, we may hear in this question the voice of Esther's autobiographical creator, for whom the prognosis is dark indeed. Like the adult Esther who is recreating this narrative, Sylvia Plath is married and a mother. She is also "in Europe" (no mere coincidence that Esther the narrator-character should include such reference in her comment); she has suffered ill health, and her marriage is troubled. And, as we now know, for Sylvia Plath the bell jar did "descend again." Only months after the novel was accepted for publication, its author attempted suicide for a second and final time.

CHAPTER 3

Early Poetry

F OR the purpose of discussing and analyzing Sylvia Plath's poetry, we can profitably observe the chronological grouping in which the poems naturally and appropriately arrange themselves. The work of any poet, of course, reveals both subtle and significant change as it progresses from early to late, from experimentation to maturity; Sylvia Plath's work is no exception. Her poetry, however, lends itself especially well to close chronological scrutiny, for her thematic concerns remain relatively constant throughout; Ted Hughes, Plath's poet husband, reminds us "how faithfully her separate poems build up into one long poem."[1] The principal changes in Plath's poetry are technical and structural, moving from the experimental quality of the early group through the transitional quality of the middle group to the mastery of the late. The reader who seeks full understanding of Plath's excellent late poems is well advised to examine first the earlier foundation upon which that work is built.

Plath's early poetry is collected principally in *The Colossus;* of her four published volumes, this is the only one which appeared during her lifetime. The contents of the British edition of this volume (published in 1960 as *The Colossus and Other Poems*) and the American edition (published in 1962) differ slightly; ten of the poems in the English volumes do not appear in the American. These poems, "Black Rook in Rainy Weather," "The Beast," "Dark House," "Maenad," "Maudlin," "Who," "Metaphors," "Ouija," "Two Sisters of Persephone," and "Witch Burning," are included, instead, in the later American volume *Crossing the Water* (1971). Nevertheless, these poems do belong to Sylvia Plath's early period, and should be considered as such. They, with the other *Colossus* poems, were written between 1955, when Plath first went to Cambridge as a Fulbright scholar, and 1959, when she toured the United States in preparation for her permanent return to England.

Ted Hughes's very helpful notes in "The Chronological Order of Sylvia Plath's Poems" permits us specifically to date the composition of most of these *Colossus* poems. One group was written between 1955 and 1957, during Plath's two years at Cambridge. Specifically, "Faun," "Strumpet Song," "Spinster," "All the Dead Dears," and "Watercolor of Grantchester Meadows" belong to Plath's first year at Cambridge; "Departure" was written in Benidorm, Spain, during the summer following Plath's marriage to Hughes; and "Hardcastle Crags" and "Sow" were inspired by Plath's visit to the home of Hughes's parents in West Yorkshire. A second group was written during 1957–1958, the year of Plath's return from England to teach English at Smith College; a visit to Cape Cod in the summer of 1957 produced "Mussel Hunter at Rock Harbor"; "The Thin People," "Lorelei," "Full Fathom Five," "Frog Autumn," "The Disquieting Muses," "Snakecharmer," "The Ghost's Leavetaking," "Sculptor," and "Night Shift" were written during the following year in Northampton, Massachusetts. Plath wrote a third group of poems during 1958–1959, when she and her husband lived on Boston's Beacon Hill; these are "The Eye-Mote," "The Man in Black," "The Hermit at Outermost House," "The Beekeeper's Daughter," "Point Shirley," "Aftermath," "Two Views of a Cadaver Room," and "Suicide Off Egg Rock." Finally, "Blue Moles," "The Winter Ship," "Mushrooms," "The Burnt-out Spa," "The Manor Garden," and the "Poem for a Birthday" sequence ("Who," "Dark House," "Maenad," "The Beast," "Flute Notes from a Reedy Pond," "Witch Burning," and "The Stones") were written during the fall of 1959 at Yaddo, following Plath's summer trip across the United States and just before her return to England.

This leaves thirteen of the fifty poems which appear in the longer British edition of *The Colossus* unaccounted for, but we can ascertain from their original dates of publication that they do indeed belong in this early period. "Two Sisters of Persephone" was first published in 1957; "The Companionable Ills," "The Times Are Tidy," "The Bull of Bendylaw," and "I Want, I Want" in 1959; and "The Colossus," "The Beast," "Maudlin," "Ouija," "Moonrise," "Who," and "Medallion" in 1960. "Metaphors" also was first published in 1960 as "Metaphors for a Pregnant Woman."

Of course, there are among the poems of Sylvia Plath's early period a number which she chose not to include in *The Colossus*. She wrote poetry from a very early age, and she composed the first

Colossus poems when she was twenty-three. There are many poems, then, which belong to the fairly substantial pre-*Colossus* period, and there are, as well, several poems written between 1955 and 1959 but not collected in the early volume. Since a number of these poems (together with some later poems) are collected in two limited-edition volumes, *Crystal Gazer* and *Lyonnesse*, published in 1971 by London's Rainbow Press, and since each poem in these volumes is followed by its date of composition, it is possible to date the early, non-*Colossus* poems which will be discussed in this chapter. These are "Admonitions" and "Dream of the Hearse-Driver," written in 1950–1951; "Mad Girl's Love Song," written in 1951; "Circus in Three Rings" and "Lament," written in 1951–1952; "Metamorphoses of the Moon," written in 1953; "Crystal Gazer," "Tinker Jack and the Tidy Wives," and "Wreath for a Bridal," written in 1956; "A Winter's Tale," written in 1958; and "The Other Two," written in 1959. Finally, Sylvia Plath's own commentary about her work, included in *Letters Home*, permits us to date the composition of three other non-*Colossus* poems with which this chapter shall deal. These poems, written during Plath's undergraduate days at Smith College, are "To Eva Descending the Stair" (1954), "Doomsday" (1954), and "Temper of Time" (1955).

Sylvia Plath's early poetry is both technically and thematically significant, for scattered through the early poems are most of the elements which were later fused into the final, powerful outbursts of the mature poetry. We find in this early work the sense of doom, the fascination with disintegration and death so central to the later poems, though the poet's expressed attitudes are less cogent, less specific in the early poems. We see as well the ambivalence toward sex, wifehood, and motherhood. The propensity to nightmare is here, too, as are many initial uses of the later, more skilfully handled, set of images.

When viewed as part of her entire canon, Sylvia Plath's early poetry displays a distinctly amateur, experimental quality. In contrast with the spontaneous, raw force of her late work, Plath's early poems seem generally contrived, mannered, and self-conscious, features apparently caused by her tendency to create artificial divisions in the essentially single dilemma she faces in these poems and by her reluctance to confront directly the various difficult subjects with which she deals. In the sense that the poet's expressed perceptions in these works appear generally less well informed than they do in

the later poems, the poetry suffers from too little control, and in the
sense that content sometimes seems artificially manipulated to fit a
set structure they suffer from too much.

I *Doom and Resistance: A Precarious Balance*

Virtually all of the early poetry is death-directed. The sense of
impending doom is often couched in somber terms, and death waits
in a diffuse gothic landscape:

> An ill wind is stalking
>   while evil stars whir
> and all the gold apples
>   go bad to the core.
> . . . .
>
> Through closets of copses
>   tall skeletons walk
> while nightshade and nettles
>   tangle the track.
> . . . .
>
> His wife and his children
>   hand riddled with shot,
> there's a hex on the cradle
>   and death in the pot.[2]

Yet, as in this poem, the gothicism seems frequently imposed for
effect rather than included by necessity. Thus, in much of Plath's
early work, the vague sense of doom is not always given an origin;
rather, nature is presented as menacing, as antipathetic to man in a
very general, undefined way:

> The figs on the fig tree in the yard are green;
> Green, also, the grapes on the green vine
> Shading the brickred porch tiles.
> The money's run out.
>
> How nature, sensing this, compounds her bitters.
> Ungifted, ungrieved, our leavetaking.
> . . . .

> The scraggy rock spit shielding the town's blue bay
> Against which the brunt of outer sea
> Beats, is brutal endlessly.[3]

If we use other available information as a gloss, however, some of the poetic references may yield more meaning and perhaps more power. In *The Bell Jar*, Esther Greenwood is profoundly affected by a story of a fig tree. She later imagines each fig to represent a direction her life might take: "I saw my life branching out before me like the green fig tree in the story," and yet she feels powerless to act or to choose: "I saw myself sitting in the crotch of this fig tree, starving to death, just because I couldn't make up my mind which of the figs I would choose. I wanted each and every one of them, but choosing one meant losing all the rest, and, as I sat there, unable to decide, the figs began to wrinkle and go black, and, one by one, they plopped to the ground at my feet" (*B*, 84, 85).

Still, in many of the early poems, the poet's attitude toward the inevitability of death is ambivalent, revealing sometimes resignation, sometimes fear, sometimes regret, and sometimes decided resistance. Though she can state that "The money's run out," or that "there's death in the pot," the poems do not quite convince us that she really means it.

In fact, this very unconvincing quality of some of the early poems reveals a tendency which distinguishes them from the late. In a few of the early works, Sylvia Plath expresses a number of positive, optimistic attitudes quite absent from her later poetry. For example, the very early villanelle "Lament" is the poet's lament for the death of her father. Although the father is represented in this poem as the imposing, colossal figure of such later (but still "early") poems as "The Colossus," "Man in Black," and "The Beekeeper's Daughter," he is not awarded the threatening, tyrannical posture of those poems. The poet's implicit attitude in "Lament" is one not of dread, but of admiration:

> The sting of bees took away my father
> Who walked in a swarming shroud of wings
> And scorned the tick of the falling weather.
> . . . .

> Trouncing the sea like a raging bather,
>   He rode the flood in a pride of prongs
> And scorned the tick of the falling weather.
>
> . . . .
>
> O ransack the four winds and find another
>   Man who can mangle the grin of kings:
> The sting of bees took away my father
> Who scorned the tick of the falling weather.[4]

Similarly, and relatedly, the poet's attitude toward marriage in some of the early poems is far more sanguine than in the later ones. In a poem composed at the commencement of her own marriage, Plath writes:

> From this holy day on, all pollen blown
> Shall strew broadcast so rare a seed on wind
> That every breath, thus teeming, set the land
> Sprouting fruit, flowers, children most fair in legion
> To slay spawn of dragon's teeth: speaking this promise,
> Let flesh be knit, and each step hence go famous.[5]

The fantastic puns in this poem seem to lend a slightly ironic edge to the tone; still, the attitude remains one of hope and blessing. In other poems, the threat suggested here by "spawn of dragon's teeth" figures more heavily, yet the possibility of failure does not obliterate the belief in success. In "The Other Two," for instance, though the married pair is happy, they are dogged by their doom-doubles:

> We dreamed their arguments, their stricken voices.
> We might embrace, but those two never did,
> Come, so unlike us, to a stiff impasse,
> Burdened in such a way we seemed the lighter—
> Ourselves the haunters and they, flesh and blood;
> As if, above love's ruinage, we were
> The heaven those two dreamed of, in despair.[6]

And in "Crystal Gazer," the gypsy who promises good fortune to the newlyweds has herself been doomed in love, Faust-like, for her passion "To govern more sight than given to a woman/ By wits alone." She sees:

> Each love blazing blind to its gutted end—
> And, fixed in the crystal center, grinning fierce:
> Earth's ever-green death's head. [7]

On other subjects as well, Plath creates in these early poems a balance between confident and cynical attitudes. The villanelle "Admonitions" states a cautionary theme similar to that of "Crystal Gazer," but with broader application:

> From here the moon seems smooth as angel-food,
>   from here you can't see spots upon the sun;
> never try to know more than you should.
> . . . .
>
> For deadly secrets strike when understood
>   and lucky stars all exit on the run:
> never try to knock on rotten wood,
> never try to know more than you should. [8]

And, expanding on the moon example of "Admonitions," the poem "Metamorphoses of the Moon" strikes a similar theme:

> The choice between the mica mystery
> of moonlight or the pockmarked face we see
>   through the scrupulous telescope
> is always to be made: innocence
> is a fairy-tale; intelligence
> hangs itself on its own rope. [9]

To be sure, optimism is not rampant in any of these poems, which seem to have a damned-if-you-do-and-damned-if-you-don't attitude. Still, there remains a hope that the damning is not inevitable. Further, it is noteworthy that in the very early poem, "Metamorphoses of the Moon" (1953), the moon has not yet come to reflect the deathlight of even the later early poetry. Perhaps what we see here is indeed a kind of metamorphosis; the moonlight's imagistic role as the light of deception in this poem could well be the logical predecessor of its later, familiar role as the cold light of blankness and death.

In fact, the moon does assume that more familiar meaning in the early poem "Hardcastle Crags." Here, as in other early poems, the poet expresses quite simultaneously her anticipation of inevitable doom and her urge to resist that inevitability. The woman in "Hardcastle Crags," taking a night walk in that stony, flinty landscape, turns away from the black indifference which threatens her there:

> before the weight
> Of stones and hills of stones could break
> Her down to mere quartz grit in that stony light
> She turned back.

This resistance, this self-preserving instinct, is a significant feature of the early poems. And even where the poet shuns positive resistance to death or disintegration, she maintains in a number of poems a perspective less evident in her final work. In "Lorelei," though the speaker finally cannot resist the sirens' song, she can recognize the madness and destructiveness of it:

> Sisters, your song
> Bears a burden too weighty
> For the whorled ear's listening
> . . . .
>
> Deranging by harmony
> Beyond the mundane order,
> Your voices lay seige.

And in "Black Rook in Rainy Weather," the poet still desires, nearly expects, the mundane order to provide flashes of significance—epiphanies, perhaps—if not design:

> I only know that a rook
> Ordering its black feathers can so shine
> As to seize my senses, haul
> My eyelids up, and grant
>
> A brief respite from fear
> Of total neutrality.[10]

There appears in this early work, then, a tension between death's allure and the poet's instinctive resistance to it. Certainly, resistance is most often momentary and impulsive, the desire for it being in some way overpowered by the claims of doom. Still, the balance between the claims of life and death, of self-preservation and destruction, is more even in the early poems than in the later ones.

Nevertheless, the quality of menace is ubiquitous in the early work, and it emanates everywhere from a natural landscape which is by turns inhospitable or threatening. Nearly any aspect of nature can serve as the agent of doom; often, as in "Lorelei," "Suicide Off Egg Rock," "Full Fathom Five," "Mussel Hunter at Rock Harbor," or "Man in Black," or as in "Point Shirley," the sea is death's agent:

> Steadily the sea
> Eats at Point Shirley. She died blessed,
> And I come by
> Bones, bones only, pawed and tossed,
> A dog-faced sea.
> The sun sinks under Boston, bloody red. ("Point Shirley")

But menace may lurk, as well, in a flinty landscape ("Hardcastle Crags"), a museum relic ("All the Dead Dears"), a pair of dead moles ("Blue Moles"), a season of the year ("Frog Autumn"), or even an aggressive crop of new mushrooms: "We shall by morning/ Inherit the earth./ Our foot's in the door" ("Mushrooms").

It is less my intent, however, to specify the sources of menace and death in these early poems than simply to recognize that these qualities form a consistent, unremitting ground bass throughout the works. The threat does indeed emanate in part from the sea, from the land, or from some vague natural or inanimate source. But whatever the origin, menace and danger remain a constant preoccupation—danger to Plath not only from external sources, but danger to her from herself. "Suicide Off Egg Rock" relates a man's successful suicide attempt:

> Behind him the hotdogs split and drizzled
> On the public grills, and the ochreous salt flats,
> Gas tanks, factory stacks—that landscape
> Of imperfections his bowels were part of—
> Rippled and pulsed in the glassy updraught.
> Sun struck the water like a damnation.
> No pit of shadow to crawl into,
> And his blood beating the old tattoo
> I am, I am, I am.

Everything shrank in the sun's corrosive
Ray but Egg Rock on the blue wastage.
He heard when he walked into the water

The forgetful surf creaming on those ledges.

When we compare these lines with an episode in *The Bell Jar*, we
may surmise that this particular danger is one to which the poet
herself feels fatally drawn. Esther Greenwood relates the events of a
day of swimming at the beach with her companions Cal, Jody, and
Mark:

A smoke seemed to be going up from my nerves like the smoke from the
grills and the sun-saturated road. The whole landscape—beach and head-
land and sea and rock—quavered in front of my eyes like a stage
backcloth. . . .
I thought I would swim out until I was too tired to swim back. As I
paddled on, my heartbeat boomed like a dull motor in my ears.
I am I am I am. . . .
I paddled my hands in the water and kicked my feet. The egg-shaped
rock didn't seem to be any nearer than it had been when Cal and I had
looked at it from the shore. . . .
The only thing to do was to drown myself then and there. (*B,* 176–80)

A closer look at a few specific poems will afford a clearer understanding of not only the quality of menace but also the concrete,
individual ways in which that quality is rendered. "The Manor Garden," for example, presents a kind of monologue in which the pregnant mother poignantly warns her baby that death and difficulty are
conditions to which he is to be born. This work, which anticipates
such later poems as "Morning Song," "You're," and "Balloons," is
one of the best in *Colossus;* its metaphors are marvelously precise
and its knitting of images affords a fine balance among the mother's
feelings of love, regret, and dread:

The fountains are dry and the roses over.
Incense of death. Your day approaches.
The pears fatten like little buddhas.
A blue mist is dragging the lake.
. . . .
You inherit white heather, a bee's wing,

> Two suicides, the family wolves,
> Hours of blankness.
> . . . .
> The small birds converge, converge
> with their gifts to a difficult borning.

Another poem, "Two Views of a Cadaver Room," anticipates the later "Death & Co." with its two—predator and lover—faces of death. Also one of the finest poems in *Colossus*, "Two Views" describes in its first section a girl's visit to "the dissecting room":

> The day she visited the dissecting room
> They had four men laid out, black as burnt turkey,
> Already half unstrung. A vinegary fume
> Of the death vats clung to them;
> The white-smocked boys started working.
> The head of his cadaver had caved in,
> And she could scarcely make out anything
> In that rubble of skull plates and old leather.
> A sallow piece of string held it together.
>
> In their jars the snail-nosed babies moon and glow.
> He hands her the cut-out heart like a cracked heirloom.

and in its second section a Breughel painting:

> In Brueghel's panorama of smoke and slaughter
> Two people only are blind to the carrion army:
> . . . .
> These Flemish lovers flourish; not for long.
>
> Yet desolation, stalled in paint, spares the little country
> Foolish, delicate, in the lower right-hand corner.

As M. L. Rosenthal observes, this whole poem reveals "some flashes of the long-standing imminence in Sylvia Plath of her final kind of awareness," especially in the "macabre" tenth line ("In their jars . . .") of the first section "with its grisly echo of Prufrock."[11] It is interesting to note also that this image of death is one which deeply impresses Esther Greenwood in *The Bell Jar*. In Chapter 6 she describes an experience nearly identical with the first section of the poem, during a tour, with Buddy Willard, of a cadaver room in his medical school. And elsewhere, Esther comments: "I thought drowning must be the kindest way to die, and burning the worst. Some of those babies in the jars that Buddy Willard showed me had gills, he said" (*B*, 177).

Closely related to this figure is the image of death explored in "Medallion." If the speaker holds a "cut-out heart" in "Two Views of a Cadaver Room," in "Medallion" she holds a dead snake, which glitters in the sun. The later associations of death with glitter are obvious in this poem. And we see here as well an early expression of Plath's association of death with chastity and perfection (evident in such *Ariel* poems as "Edge," "Fever 103°," and "A Birthday Present"): "Knifelike, he was chaste enough,/ Pure death's metal. The yardman's/ Flung brick perfected his laugh."

A different kind of attitude toward death is presented in "To Eva Descending the Stair," a villanelle in which word order sometimes seems tampered with for the sake of rhyme. Here the menace comes not from tangible nature but from time, and the poet indicates that time, even though it may be destructive, has not yet stopped: "Clocks cry: stillness is a lie, my dear;/ The wheels revolve, the universe keeps running./ Proud you halt upon the spiral stair."[12] But if "clocks cry" and "stillness," the condition of death in the later poetry, "is a lie" at one moment, time crashingly halts at another:

> Too late to ask if end was worth the means,
> Too late to calculate the toppling stock:
> The idiot bird leaps out and drunken leans.
> The hour is crowed in lunatic thirteens.[13]

Thematically, this poem points toward the final "too late" poems. And it is an early example of the hallucinatory, surreal quality of expression which becomes a mannerism in the poet's later work.

It is interesting to observe at this point, that while Plath does experiment in the early poems with the surrealist style she uses so effectively in the late work, she also explores the contents and materials of that mode. As surrealist art celebrates the mind's free operation, and exploits, in part, the material of nightmare and dream and the mind's state between sleeping and waking, so Sylvia Plath examines, in her early work, the actual content of dreams. In "The Dream of the Hearse-Driver," the driver himself describes his dreaming of the previous night:

> "Last night," he said, "I slept well
> except for two uncanny dreams
> ....
> "In the first dream I was driving
> down the dark in a black hearse
> with many men until I crashed
> a light, and right away a raving
> woman followed us and rushed
> to halt our car in headlong course.
> ....
> "Behind me then I heard a voice
> warning me to hold her hand
> and kiss her on the mouth for she
> loved me and a brave embrace
> would avoid all penalty.
> 'I know, I know,' I told my friend.
> ....
> I do not tell you the nightmare
> which occurred to me in China."[14]

If Plath portrays the dream itself in "The Dream of the Hearse-Driver," she explores the time when dreams occur in "The Ghost's Leavetaking," the

> chilly no-man's land of about
> Five o'clock in the morning, the no-colour void
> Where the waking head rubbishes out the draggled lot
> Of sulphurous dreamscapes and obscure lunar conundrums
> Which seemed, when dreamed, to mean so profoundly much.

Both of these poems very skilfully capture the quality of the dream, and are highly successful in their exploration and evocation of the dream state. And, significantly, they indicate a direction Plath chose to abandon in her later poems—that of writing about the surrealist region of dream and nightmare, of the margin between waking and sleep, rather than of writing from that region.

Apparent in these early poems, then, are several features uncharacteristic of Plath's later work. Her emphasis on the sleeping, dreaming state as a region separate from the waking one is evident only in the early work; later, she adroitly, and terrifyingly, combines the two. And the whimsical, and sometimes desperate, optimism of some of the early poems is an attitude later abandoned.

Nevertheless, this optimism does not dominate even the early work, which is characterized generally by a wavering attitude toward time coupled with an abiding sense of doom. Sometimes, however, the brooding, gothic atmosphere and the general pronouncements of doom are replaced by a sort of wild defiance which, though surreal, goes far beyond the surrealism of "Doomsday" or "Temper of Time." In these poems, even though they often seem verbally stilted and structurally forced, it is possible to detect the beginning of an energy bordering on hysteria which points directly to the later poems. It is interesting to compare some of these madly energetic lines with an excerpt from a short autobiographical sketch of Sylvia Plath entitled "Ocean 1212-W" (1963), a sketch in which Plath recorded a number of impressions of the first nine years of her life on Cape Cod: "My final memory of the sea is of violence—a still, unhealthily yellow day in 1939, the sea molten, . . . heaving at its leash like a broody animal. . . . My brother and I . . . imbibed the talk of tidal waves . . . like a miracle elixir. This was a monstrous specialty, a leviathan. Our world might be eaten, blown to bits. We wanted to be on it. . . . The only sound was a howl, jazzed up by the bangs, slams, groans, and splintering of objects tossed like crockery in a giant's quarrel."[15]

> In the circus tent of a hurricane
> designed by a drunken god
> my extravagant heart blows up again
> in a rampage of champagne-colored rain
> and the fragments whir like a weather vane
> while the angels all applaud. ("Circus in Three Rings")[16]

Certainly, the comparison is instructive. Not only does it help to reinforce meanings already inherent in the poetry itself and to emphasize the intensely autobiographical nature of that poetry; it also points to the way in which external and internal landscape become inseparable in the later work. In the interpretation of the child's experience we can already hear the mocking, desperate tones of Lady Lazarus.

II   *Humor*

In fact, this mocking, even occasionally humorous voice is an aspect which should be stressed in discussing Sylvia Plath's poetry.

Certainly, none of the poems is raucously funny, but subtle humor of various kinds is visible. And this is another feature which distinguishes the early work from the late; the humorous attitude of some of the early poems is one which Plath seems to have relinquished by the time she wrote her final ones. In those, levity is diminished, and bitter mockery predominates.

The early poem, "A Winter's Tale," for example, creates an amusing, almost funny, picture of the Boston Common at Christmas:

> By S. S. Pierce, by S. S. Pierce,
> The red-nosed, blue-nosed women ring
> For money. Lord, the crowds are fierce!
> There's carolling
>
> On Winter Street, on Temple Place.
> Poodles are baking cookies in
> Filene's show windows. Grant us grace,
> Donner, Blitzen.
>
> And all you Santa's deer who browse
> By leave of the Park Commission
> On grass that once fed Boston cows.[17]

Certainly the satiric tone so evident in many of Plath's later poems is here, but in this playful poem the satire is far less acrid.

In "Mushrooms," a wry, and even droll, kind of humor is achieved by rhythms:

> We are shelves, we are
> Tables, we are meek,
> We are edible,
>
> Nudgers and shovers
> In spite of ourselves.

by rhymes and word sounds:

> Overnight, very
> Whitely, discreetly,
> Very quietly,

> Our toes, our noses
> Take hold on the loam,
> Acquire the air.

and by the very nature of the poem's speakers and situation. Nor, as Israel Horovitz remarks, are the poem's "special sly obscenities" to be overlooked.[18]

The playfulness of the riddle and of the word game is evoked in "Metaphors," where pregnancy is the answer to the riddle, and the "nine syllables" indicate both the nine-syllable lines and the nine lines of the poem as well as the nine months of pregnancy:

> I'm a riddle in nine syllables,
> An elephant, a ponderous house,
> A melon strolling on two tendrils.
> O red fruit, ivory, fine timbers!
> This loaf's big with its yeasty rising.
> Money's new-minted in this fat purse.
> I'm a means, a stage, a cow in calf.
> I've eaten a bag of green apples,
> Boarded the train there's no getting off.[19]

The train image here suggests none of the death-driven necessity of such later, similar images, as in "Getting There" and "Years." Yet, as it signifies birth and new life, the railroad image of "Metaphors" does point toward the death-car of the late poems, anticipating the theme of birth-death fusion so central to Plath's final vision.

Still another kind of humor, the black, sardonic humor achieved so effectively in the late poem "Lady Lazarus," is evident in the early work. We can recognize that mocking voice, which manages to ridicule both speaker and audience, not only in "Circus in Three Rings" but also in "Tinker Jack and the Tidy Wives":

> "Come lady, bring that pot
> Gone black of polish
> And whatever pan this mending master
> Should trim back to shape;
> I'll correct each mar
> On silver dish,
> And shine that kettle of copper
> Bright as blood."[20]

Thus, Plath's use of the comic mode in this early work reveals one direction that her poetry might have taken, and one that it did take. The jocularity evident in the early vision seems a quality which had no place in the late. To be sure, humor is not the major distinguishing feature of the early poems; in them, Plath's humor and pessimism seem almost to alternate between poems, with one or the other aspect governing a single work—and with the menacing, pessimistic attitude predominating. But in the darker vision of the late work, the humor gives way to the more bitter satiric mode. There, the poet employs her acerbic wit in a defensive way, using comedy to create a necessary distance between her painful subjects and her personal awareness of them. In *Ariel* and *Winter Trees*, the waggishness of "A Winter's Tale," the drollery of "Mushrooms," the playfulness of "Metaphors," and the mockery of "Tinker Jack and the Tidy Wives" fuse into a single kind of defiant, bitter comedy which is essential to the power not only of "Lady Lazarus" but also of many others.

III *Conflict*

Although Plath's extreme pessimism in these early poems is not often assigned any specific cause, possible causes are suggested in the form of deeply rooted and potentially disabling emotional conflicts. From references to her father we learn that he is rigid, extremely stern, and black, and basically this is all the poet ever tells us about her father himself. It is even more revealing, however, that in all of "Ocean 1212-W," where Plath gives at least some insight into the character of her grandparents, her mother, her brother, and even her uncle, the sole mention of her father appears in the closing words: "And this is how it stiffens, my vision of that seaside childhood. My father died, we moved inland."[21]

If there is only scanty description of father, however, there is a wealth of suggestion regarding his effect on the poet's life. As seen in the passages quoted above, she feels that his stifling rule has turned her to stone. "The Colossus," title poem of her first volume, is concerned on the literal level with a broken ancient statue: "I shall never get you put together entirely,/ Pieced, glued, and properly jointed." Reference here is probably not only to her father, as the statute that "I" despairs of patching, but also to herself and her own emotional "break" approximately three years earlier. Decidedly, this poem anticipates the later "Daddy," where the Colossus figure is expanded to include also the husband, and where the poet has abandoned her patching efforts. In "The Colossus," the speaker contends that

> Thirty years not I have laboured
> To dredge the silt from your throat.
> I am none the wiser.
>
> Scaling little ladders with gluepots and pails of lysol
> I crawl like an ant in mourning
> Over the weedy acres of your brow.

But in "Daddy," she announces that "I have had to kill you." Still praying for recovery in the early work, she continues in "The Colossus":

> A blue sky out of the Oresteia
> Arches above us. O father, all by yourself
> You are pithy and historical as the Roman Forum.

Identifying with Orestes in this poem, she reaches for another parallel in "Electra on Azalea Path":

> I borrow the stilts of an old tragedy.
> The truth is, one late October, at my birth-cry
> A scorpion stung its head, an ill-starred thing;
> My mother dreamed you face down in the sea.
> . . . .
> O pardon the one who knocks for pardon at
> Your gate, father—your hound-bitch, daughter, friend.
> It was my love that did us both to death.[22]

And in "The Eye-Mote," she uses still another, similar classical reference to describe the conflict:

> I wear the present itch for flesh,
> Blind to what will be and what was.
> I dream that I am Oedipus.
>
> What I want back is what I was
> Before the bed, before the knife.

This Orestes-Electra-Oedipus person is surely the one who speaks so powerfully in such later poems as not only "Daddy" but also "Fever 103°," "Lady Lazarus," and "Little Fugue."

Indeed, this ominous Colossus figure is represented also relatively early in Sylvia Plath's work. Her award-winning short story, "Sunday at the Mintons'," published in 1952 at the end of Plath's sophomore year in college, concerns the relationship of Elizabeth Minton with her brother Henry, "a colossus astride the roaring sea."[23] The maiden Elizabeth has returned to her family home by the ocean to care for her older brother in his retirement. She has, apparently, always been dominated and bullied by him; orderly, demanding, and overbearing, Henry scorns Elizabeth's active imagination and her tendency to daydream. Now that she and Henry are together again, Elizabeth instinctively reverts to her childhood role: "a little girl, obedient and yielding."[24] Yet she finds growing within her a new attitude of defiance. In the story's denouement, Elizabeth imagines that as she and Henry take their prescribed walk near the sea following Sunday's dinner, Henry is drowned. One thing that is particularly interesting here is the cause of Henry's demise; he is doing a favor for Elizabeth—retrieving a pin she has dropped—when the sea overcomes him. Elizabeth's response to this cataclysmic event is also significant; she watches for a time in wonder, almost in delight, before she steps to join Henry in the stormy waves. Her ambivalence is complete; she is at once defiant and yielding. Elizabeth, the little girl figure, may bring death to the colossus, but she must ultimately also join him in death.

An additional contributor to these conflicts so clearly expressed in Plath's early work is the mother. This is of especial interest, since virtually no mention is made in Plath's late poetry of her mother. The only maternal figure in *Ariel* is the poet herself, and mother-child relationsnips are treated there in a loving, poignant way quite different from the modes of expression in *Colossus*.

In a number of the poems comprising "Poem for a Birthday," mother's relation to the speaker, as the speaker comprehends it, appears generally distant and unconcerned. The poem "Maenad" seems central in defining these individuals and their relationship, for the speaker does assume the character of a maenadic woman, frenzied and raging, throughout the seven-poem sequence. And the cause of the speaker's present condition is assigned, in "Maenad," largely to maternal disregard:

> The mother of mouths didn't love me.
> The old man shrank to a doll.
> O I am too big to go backward:
> ....
> Mother, keep out of my barnyard,
> I am becoming another.[25]

In a different tone, the poem "The Disquieting Muses" deals also, and in detail, with mother. The speaker here addresses her mother directly in a series of stanzas each designed to explore a particular aspect of the daughter's childhood recollections. Generally, the poet expresses here the familiar you-don't-understand-me theme of nearly every child to a parent, of nearly every daughter to a mother. But one suspects that for this speaker (as for many others), the strength of the conviction is not diminished by its lack of uniqueness:

> Mother, mother, what illbred aunt
> Or what disfigured and unsightly
> Cousin did you so unwisely keep
> Unasked to my christening, that she
> Sent these ladies in her stead
> With heads like darning-eggs to nod
> And nod and nod at foot and head
> And at the left side of my crib?
> ....
> Day now, night now, at head, side, feet,
> They stand their vigil in gowns of stone,
> Faces blank as the day I was born,
> Their shadows long in the setting sun
> That never brightens or goes down.
> And this is the kingdom you bore me to,
> Mother, mother. But no frown of mine
> Will betray the company I keep.

Further, of course, in the poems "The Colossus," "Electra on Azalea Path," and "The Eye-Mote," the daughter-father relationship is not the only one invoked as a source of conflict. Orestes, with whom the poet identifies, murdered his mother with the assistance of Electra, his sister; Oedipus' incestuous love for his mother occasioned her death.

Thus, these poems of conflict present not only an early statement

of the poet's ambivalent sexual attitudes; they foreshadow the later
poems in other ways as well. As Charles Newman observes, "clearly
the loss of the father, the ambiguous hand of the mother will remain
her central preoccupations."[26] "The Eye-Mote," especially, should
be read partly as a metaphor for Sylvia Plath's peculiar, surreal
vision, which operates only erratically in the early poems but persis-
tently in the late ones:

> Blameless as daylight I stood looking
> At a field of horses, necks bent, manes blown,
> Tails streaming against the green
> Backdrop of sycamores.
> . . . .
> When the splinter flew in and stuck in my eye,
> Needling it dark. Then I was seeing
> A melding of shapes in a hot rain:
> Horses warped on the altering green,
>
> Outlandish as double-humped camels or unicorns,
> Grazing at the margins of a bad monochrome,
> Beasts of oasis, a better time.
> Abrading my lid, the small grain burns:
> Red cinder around which I myself,
> Horses, planets and spires revolve.

The horses of this poem strongly suggest the horse Ariel galloping
toward the still point, toward "What I want," toward death.

The source of the conflicts expressed in these poems is mainly
sexual, and the manifestations of this dilemma are far-reaching. The
poems' speaker longs to be a "strumpet," a "foul slut": "Until every
man,/ Red, pale or dark,/ Veers to her slouch" ("Strumpet Song").
She yearns for the sexual abandon offered by the fantastic
snakecharmer who "Pipes water green until green waters waver/
With reedy lengths and necks and undulatings" ("Snakecharmer").
Yet her "present itch for flesh" ("The Eye-Mote") conflicts with the
"Spinster" in her:

> And round her house she set
> Such a barricade of barb and check
> Against mutinous weather
> As no mere insurgent man could hope to break
> With curse, fist, threat,
> Or love, either.

Even the tone of this poem is uncertain, thereby illustrating the conflict between strumpet and spinster shown so clearly among the other poems.

IV *Integration*

There exists, I think, a positive correlation between the poet's increasingly honest confrontation with these problems and a growing power and efficiency in her poetry; extraneous props like a cuckoo clock, a staircase, or frivolous gothicism in nature give way to mythic reference, and strumpets, stones, snakes, and spinsters are as symbolic and internal as they are real. The few poems in this early group where Plath controls together many or all of the facets of her personal dilemma instead of creating artificial divisions in it anticipate the later poetry. In "Full Fathom Five," Plath writes:

> Old man, you surface seldom.
> Then you come in with the tide's coming
> . . . .
> All obscurity
> Starts with a danger:
> Your dangers are many. I
> Cannot look much but your form suffers
> Some strange injury
>
> And seems to die. . . .

This poem, and several of the others quoted above, demonstrate the structural freedom and verbal elasticity of the mature, later work. "The Stones," the last poem in the "Poem for a Birthday" sequence and in *The Colossus*, attests to Plath's achievement of that style:

> This is the city where men are mended.
> I lie on a great anvil.
> . . . .
>
> Love is the bone and sinew of my curse.
> The vase, reconstructed, houses
> The elusive rose.
>
> Ten fingers shape a bowl for shadows.
> My mendings itch. There is nothing to do.
> I shall be as good as new.

"The Stones," then, represents both a culmination and a departure, a success afforded by the "advanced exercises" of the earlier poems. And it is interesting, and perhaps enlightening, to note that Ted Hughes, also, sees "The Stones" as a turning point in Sylvia Plath's poetic career: "THE STONES was the last poem she wrote . . . in America. The immediate source of it was a series of poems she began as a deliberate exercise in experimental improvisation on set themes. She had never in her life improvised. The powers that compelled her to write so slowly had always been stronger than she was. But quite suddenly she found herself free to let herself drop, rather than inch over bridges of concepts. . . . STONES . . . is clearly enough the first eruption of the voice that produced *Ariel*.[27]

CHAPTER 4

Transitional Poetry

IF "The Stones" is the "first eruption" of that final, excellent voice,
however, it does not herald an immediate success. There are a
number of poems which Sylvia Plath wrote between 1960 when *The
Colossus* was first published and early 1962, which may be accurately termed transitional. These poems are collected in *Crossing
the Water,* and they belong to the three-year period which followed
Plath's second visit to England. This was the time of the Hugheses'
two years in London and their first year in Devon, a period ending
roughly with the breakup of their marriage and Ted's departure
from home. It was not, on the whole, either a happy or a poetically
productive time for Plath. To be sure, her two children were born in
these years—Frieda Rebecca in 1960, and Nicholas Farrar in 1962.
But it was a period when Plath often felt choked by domesticity, as
she said, and when she suffered continuing poor health.

The poems which we may call transitional generally reveal
neither the honesty of the early poems nor the power of the late
ones. To be sure, a number of poems which properly belong to
Plath's late period were written also during this 1960–1962 period;
the distinction between "transitional" and "late" must be made on
the basis not only of composition date, but also of style and approach. Indeed, the transitional volume *Crossing the Water* is aptly
named, for the poems of this period do indeed evince, variously, a
kind of stepping-stone quality, or a sense of floundering, of being
neither on one shore nor the other. Both in form and in substance,
these poems are mainly interesting only because they are there,
because they represent an important stage in Sylvia Plath's poetic
development.

In the interest of accuracy, it should be noted that, like the early
volume *Colossus,* the contents of the British edition of *Crossing the
Water* (published in 1971, eight years after Sylvia Plath's death), and
the American edition (also published in 1971) differ slightly. The ten

57

early poems which failed to appear in the American *Colossus* are printed in the American version of *Crossing the Water*. And, because of space problems perhaps, there are six transitional poems in the English volume which do not appear in the American. These poems: "Pheasant," "An Appearance," "Event," "Apprehensions," "The Tour," and "Among the Narcissi," are included instead in the American edition of *Winter Trees*. By their nature, however, these six poems do belong to Plath's transitional period and they shall be treated here as such.

We can date the actual composition of thirteen of these thirty-four transitional poems with the aid of *Crystal Gazer* and *Lyonnesse* (both published in 1971), the "Six Poems" published in *The New Yorker* in 1971, and the poems which appear in the "Appendix" to *The Art of Sylvia Plath*, all of which provide their poems' composition dates. According to these sources, "Two Campers in Cloud Country" was written in 1960; "Face Lift," "Heavy Women," "The Babysitters," "In Plaster," "Leaving Early," "Widow," "Mirror," "Zoo Keeper's Wife," and "Last Words" were composed in 1961; and "Pheasant," "An Appearance," and "Apprehensions" were written in 1962. Of the remaining poems of the thirty-four appearing in the more complete Faber edition of *Crossing the Water*, eighteen were first published during 1960–1962; these, then, may be considered part of this group because of their publication dates as well as because of their transitional quality. They are "Candles," published in 1960; "Parliament Hill Fields," "Insomniac," "I Am Vertical," "Private Ground," "Magi," "Small Hours," "Sleep in the Mojave Desert," "A Life," "On Deck," and "Whitsun," published in 1961; and "Wuthering Heights," "Crossing the Water," "Finisterre," "Blackberrying," "Event," "Love Letter," and "The Surgeon at 2 a.m.," published in 1962. This leaves only three poems—"Among the Narcissi" (first published posthumously in 1963), and "The Tour" and "Stillborn" (both first published in 1971)—unaccounted for. By their treatments of theme and their subjects, these three poems may be accurately said to belong to this middle period. "Stillborn" is an especially typical and significant transitional poem, as we shall see.

I   *Structural Transitions*

The work of Sylvia Plath's transitional period reveals, in several ways, the poet's continuing effort to achieve her own style. For one

thing, the stepping-stone quality of these transitional poems is revealed in their structure; the mutation in Plath's use of rhymes,
rhythms, sounds, and stanza forms from the early to the late poems
is a process instructive to follow in tracing her gradual achievement
of economical expression. John Frederick Nims accurately, and
closely, describes the differences in these specific components in
the *Colossus* and *Ariel* poems; he observes a "less obtrusive" attention to sound effects and at the same time a stronger emphasis on
"ghostly," irregular end rhymes in *Ariel*, a more obvious attention to
short stanzas combined with a near abandonment of formal end-
rhyme and stanza constructions, and a change from metrical experimentation in *Colossus* to an almost exclusive use of iambs in
Ariel.[1]

We can see these changes occurring in the transitional poems. In
stanza form, the early poems are far more conventionally structured
than the late, and a partial survey simply of the kinds of stanza
structures which Plath progressively employs reveals the tendency
of her poetry toward greater structural freedom and verbal elasticity. For example, in the early poems there are five villanelles and
one sestina, but there are none among the transitional or late works.
Further, in *The Colossus*, twelve poems are written in three-line
stanzas of which six are terza rima. In *Crossing the Water*, of seven
poems written in three-line stanzas, only three are terza rima. In
Ariel, there are no terza rima constructions in the eleven poems
written in three-line stanzas. Throughout her work, then, Plath
apparently feels comfortable writing in three-line stanzas; she re-
tains this structure, but moves away from her early employment of
the highly schematized terza rima and villanelle toward use of a
freer three-line form.

This movement toward flexibility and brevity can be dramatized
also by simply cataloging different stanza lengths in Plath's early,
transitional, and late work. *The Colossus* contains one poem written
in two-line units with irregular end-rhyme; *Crossing the Water* has
none; *Ariel* has nine. In *The Colossus* there are eleven poems in
four-line stanzas, eight poems in five-line stanzas, and seventeen
poems in stanzas of six or more lines; *Crossing the Water* contains no
four-line and six five-line stanza poems, and twenty poems in stanzas of six or more lines; in *Ariel*, three of the poems are written in
four-line stanzas, fifteen in five-line, and only five in stanzas of six or
more lines. After experimentation in long stanzas, then, Plath gen-

erally returns in her late work to shorter, more economical, and more flexible stanza forms.

The trend is toward a simpler, more direct, and more emphatic verse. This same trend may be observed in Plath's use of rhythms and diction. Nims observes that the predominant metrical pattern of *The Colossus* is the syllabic line, the nearly exclusive pattern in *Ariel* is the iambic. The poems in *Crossing the Water* are written in the earlier mode. The diction of *Colossus*, says Nims, "is always distinguished and elegant, but is "a written language rather than a spoken one." In *Ariel*, on the other hand, we hear "a real voice in a real body in a real world."[2] Again, *Crossing the Water* belongs more to the *Colossus* than to the *Ariel* category.

This change in Sylvia Plath's poems from a written to a spoken language is one observed not only by a number of critics but also by the poet herself. Douglas Cleverdon suggests that Plath's composition of the voice play *Three Women*, and her experience in broadcasting this and other poetry over the BBC from 1960 on, may well have marked the turning point between poems not meant to be read aloud, and poems intended to be.[3] A. Alvarez, too, observes a difference "between finger-count" in Plath's early poems and "ear-count" in the late; "one measures the rhythm by rules," he contends, while "the other catches the movement by the inner disturbance it creates."[4] On this subject, we may indeed invoke the poet herself, who, in a 1962 interview and reading of her own work, claimed that designing her poems to be effective when read aloud "is something I didn't do in my earlier poems. For example, my first book, *The Colossus*, I can't read any of the poems aloud now. I didn't write them to be read aloud. . . . These ones . . . that are very recent, I've got to say them, I speak them to myself, and I think that this in my own writing development is quite a new thing with me, and whatever lucidity they may have comes from the fact that I say them to myself, I say them aloud."[5]

This observation is certainly accurate. Because of their syntax, for one thing, a number of Plath's early poems yield very reluctantly to being read aloud. The Petrarchan sonnet "Mayflower" (1955) offers one example of this unwieldy syntactical aspect in the early work. In it, the occasional dropping of the definite and indefinite article lends a jerky, abrupt quality to the line flow—not the calculated, effective abruptness of such late poems as "Lady Lazarus," but a disrupting jerkiness which requires distracting pauses in the reading:

> Throughout black winter the red haws withstood
> Assault of snow-flawed winds from the dour skies
> And, bright as blood-drops, proved no brave branch dies
> If root's firm-fixed and resolution good. . . .[6]

Other early poems, such as "Wreath for a Bridal" (1956), offer either a similar sort of disruptive ellipsis, or unexpected syntactical inversions, so that the reader becomes at times unsure of the function of certain words: "Now speak some sacrament to parry scruple/ For wedlock wrought within love's proper chapel."[7] "The Goring" (1956) offers similar difficulty: "Arena dust rusted by four bulls' blood to a dull redness,/. . ./ Instinct for art began with the bull's horn lofting in the mob's/ Hush a lumped man-shape."[8] This crowding of words and figures which requires such deliberate, careful reading is, of course, not in itself a flawed technique. Such a poetic style can be highly effective—as used, for example, by Dylan Thomas. But, although Sylvia Plath experiments with this technique in her early work, she later discards it for a more natural, spoken cadence. By the time of the transitional poems, Plath employs a much smoother syntax.

This change in oral quality from Plath's early to her late work is observable not only in the poems' syntax, but in their employment of diction and sound as well. As Nims points out, "the sound of words—any page of Sylvia Plath shows her preoccupation with it. *The Colossus* shows a concern almost excessive, unless we see it as a preparation for *Ariel*."[9] In this aspect as in most of the others, the *Crossing the Water* poems indicate transition. A reader is almost constantly aware in the early poems of technical experimentation, especially in sound (and in related diction); there, sound effects are often effective, and often impressive, but often, as well, obtrusive:

> And he within this snakedom
>
> Rules the writhings which make manifest
> His snakehood and his might with plaint tunes
> From his thin pipe.
>
> Hard gods were there, nothing else.
> Still he thumbed out something else.
> Thumbed no stony, horny pot,
> But a certain meaning green.[10]

By the time of the late poems, this tongue-twisting quality is abandoned; diction is more natural, words are more easily spoken, sound
effects are more appropriate, and the line-flow is more economical.
This change is already occurring in the transitional poems. There,
Plath continues her experimentation with internal rhymes, and
with alliteration, assonance, and consonance. But the effects
throughout are less obtrusive than in the earlier poems—sometimes
only slightly less so, as in the transitional "Insomniac":

> The night sky is only a sort of carbon paper,
> Blueblack, with the much-poked periods of stars
> Letting in the light, peephole after peephole—
> A bonewhite light, like death, behind all things.[11]

and more often decidedly less so, as in "Event":

> The moonlight, that chalk cliff
> In whose rift we lie
>
> Back to back. I hear an owl cry
> From its cold indigo.[12]

This transitional experimentation points toward the two very different sound aspects of the late poems; Plath's increasing control over
her sound effects in *Crossing the Water* allows not only the powerful
subtlety of such late poems as "The Moon and the Yew Tree" or
"Little Fugue," but also the effective and obvious rhymes of such
poems as "Lady Lazarus" and "Daddy."

II *Cut-paper People*

In all aspects of form, then, the transitional poems reveal the
changes from the early to the late ones. At the same time, they seem
peculiarly lifeless. Indeed, what is significant about them is their
very quality of literariness and of falseness to real experience.
Though it is true that the early poems seem often artificially contrived, they nonetheless manage to evince, sometimes, a kind of raw
force. It is not the disciplined, controlled power of the late poems,
where, to quote Richard Wilbur's comment on poetry in general,
"the strength of the genie comes of his being confined in a bottle."[13]
But a real voice does break through in such early poems as "The

Stones," or "Full Fathom Five," or "The Eye-Mote," or "Two Views of a Cadaver Room." We hear this real voice seldom in *Crossing the Water*.

Two poems in this transitional collection seem to express the nature of the whole group. One is the title poem, "Crossing the Water," beginning

> Black lake, black boat, two black, cut-paper people.
> Where do the black trees go that drink here?
> Their shadows must cover Canada.

To the reader this poem, and most of the other poems of this period, are like the figures described in this scene—they are colorless, two-dimensional, and have a cut-from-paper quality.

Helen Vendler makes a similar observation. "The withdrawal of affect," she writes, "annihilates not only nature but people." She uses the examples of "Two Campers in Cloud Country" and "Whit-sun" to show that people are no more than "stick-figures," and she comments further that "Face-Lift" reveals a "falseness to the wellsprings of life from which metaphors are drawn." The main problem with the poems in this volume, says Vendler, is that "an undeniable intellect allegorizes the issues before they are allowed expression."[14]

Clearly, Plath's ability, newfound in her composition of "The Stones," to "let herself drop, rather than inch over bridges of concepts," has not yet emerged as a consistent mannerism in these transitional peoms. The apparent spontaneity of her late poems, which accounts for so much of their power, is largely absent here. About the *Colossus* poems one might say, generally, that the forced, stylized quality results from the poet's vigorous experimentation with the materials of her craft. In the transitional poems, however, the lack of spontaneity appears to result rather from an almost total self-consciousness on the poet's part.

Two manifestations of this self-consciousness in *Crossing the Water* are the surprisingly undramatic quality of the poems and the comparatively large number of landscape poems. In both the earlier and the later poetry, the speaker assumes an identifiable voice, an individual identity, so that the poems themselves present a clear dramatic situation. In *The Colossus*, for example, we hear the voice of a woman agonizingly confronting the sirens' temptation, or the

voice of a daughter trying to come to terms with a very specific
father relationship, or the voice of a proliferating mushroom family,
or the voice of a spinster shakily committed to self-denial. Even in
the landscape poems, like "Hardcastle Crags" or "Point Shirley,"
the speaker is given a special identity, and is surrounded by that
particular, believable landscape for a particular and evident reason.

In *Ariel*, the same dramatic concreteness prevails. Here, there
are virtually no landscape poems, in the previous sense of an
identifiable natural setting for the speaker's activities. For by this
time, external settings have become internalized so that they serve
only as functions of the speaker's peculiar or distorted vision. (For
example, moonlight in "The Moon and the Yew Tree" becomes "the
light of the mind," and golden apples and leaves and flowers in
"Letter in November" are "the mouths of Thermopylae.") And
throughout the volume, the identifiable speaker acts and talks in a
clear dramatic context—a Jew victimized by a Nazi, for example, or
a mother poignantly warning her child of his probable fate, or an
onion-chopping housewife cutting her thumb.

But in *Crossing the Water*, we find very little dramatic concreteness and hear mainly an amorphous voice. We might, in fact, take
the first stanza of "Magi," a poem from this volume, as evidence of
this failure of realization:

> The abstracts hover like dull angels:
> Nothing so vulgar as a nose or eye
> Bossing the ethereal blanks of their face-ovals.

In *Crossing the Water*, the poet seems sharply conscious of herself,
so that her poems' characters and situations remain more or less
abstract.

For example, there are among these transitional works more
landscape poems than appear proportionately in the work of the
other periods. In them, the speaker is "I," and "I" is occasionally
accompanied by a "you." Generally one has the impression that "I"
and "you" and the surrounding landscape exist to express an idea
the poet has—an idea, which, struggling for expression, renders the
specifics of the poem subordinate and rather lifeless. In "Wuthering
Heights," for instance, both speaker and landscape evince a dis-
turbingly substanceless quality:

The horizons ring me like faggots,
Tilted and disparate, and always unstable.
Touched by a match, they might warm me,
And their fine lines singe
The air to orange
Before the distances they pin evaporate,
Weighting the pale sky with a solider colour.
But they only dissolve and dissolve
Like a series of promises, as I step forward.

In "Two Campers in Cloud Country," where the idea is the person's desire for self-effacement in an indifferent landscape, effacement occurs even before identity can be established:

Well, one wearies of the Public Gardens: one wants a vacation
Where trees and clouds and animals pay no notice;
(p. 32, H & R ed.)
. . . .
The Pilgrims and Indians might never have happened.
Planets pulse in the lake like bright amoebas;
The pines blot our voices up in their lightest sighs.

Similarly, characters fail to become real beings in a number of the other poems of *Crossing the Water*. "A Life," for example, seems to have both speaker and listener—someone is giving various orders to someone else—but we remain unsure of who they are or what they are doing or why they are doing it:

Touch it: it won't shrink like an eyeball,
This egg-shaped bailiwick, clear as a tear.
. . . .
Flick the glass with your fingernail:
It will ping like a Chinese chime in the slightest air stir
Though nobody in there looks up or bothers to answer.

An interesting companion to these observations is the fact that these transitional poems are quite humorless. We cannot be certain whether this characteristic is a cause, or an effect, of overintellectualization and lack of spontaneity; it is observable, however, that with a very few exceptions, these poems lack the wit, the drollery, and even the bitter, mocking humor of both the early and the late work. To be sure, there is a witty line or two, for example in "Leaving Early": "Lady, your room is lousy with flowers." (p. 18) And we can hear the humorous satire of the early poem "A Winter's Tale" in the transitional "On Deck":

> The untidy lady revivalist
> For whom the good Lord provides (He gave
> Her a pocketbook, a pearl hatpin
> And seven winter coats last August)
> Prays under her breath that she may save
> The art students in West Berlin.

or the mocking tones of early and late poems in "The Tour":

> O maiden aunt, you have come to call.
> Do step into the hall!
> . . . .
> And *this*
> Is where I kept the furnace,
> . . . .
> It simply exploded one night,
> It went up in smoke.
> And that's why I have no hair, auntie, that's why I choke.[15]

As a group, however, the transitional poems are quite sober.

Therefore, since these poems are valuable to study largely for their transitional qualities rather than their artistic success, the other poem in *Crossing the Water* which seems expressive of the whole group is "Stillborn," in which the poet herself announces her dissatisfaction with her work:

> These poems do not live: it's a sad diagnosis.
> They grew their toes and fingers well enough,
> Their little foreheads bulged with concentration.
> If they missed out on walking about like people
> It wasn't for any lack of mother-love.
>
> O I cannot understand what happened to them!
> They are proper in shape and number and every part.
> They sit so nicely in the pickling fluid!
> They smile and smile and smile and smile at me.
> And still the lungs won't fill and the heart won't start.

III   *Refinement of Imagery*

But even though the poems of this period are generally lifeless, overintellectualized, and humorless, they are valuable not only as formal transitions but as transitions in their use of imagery as well. In this group of poems, Sylvia Plath seems to have culled from the early work the relatively small group of images she will use later, and here she uses them over and over again, in various combinations. One might speculate that without this time to become totally familiar with her system of imagery, she might not have succeeded in using it as brilliantly as she does in the poems which follow.

In the poem "Private Ground," for example, we find an explanation, clearer probably than any in *Ariel*, of the meaning of the familiar death images of frost, glitter, and reflection:

> All morning, with smoking breath, the handyman
> Has been draining the goldfish ponds.
> They collapse like lungs,
> . . . .
> I bend over this drained basin where the small fish
> Flex as the mud freezes.
> They glitter like eyes, and I collect them all.
> Morgue of old logs and old images, the lake
> Opens and shuts, accepting them among its reflections.

The mirror, too, is an image which belongs to this particular group of death figures. Plath uses it in conjunction with the color white (another, related figure for death's blankness) in "Last Words": "My mirror is clouding over—/A few more breaths, and it will reflect nothing at all./ The flowers and faces whiten to a sheet." (p. 40) And in the poem "Mirror," Plath offers a detailed exploration of the special connotations this image has for her. We can recognize here the particular relation with death (and drowning) of such figures and allusions as candlelight and moonlight, silver, water, and narcissi:

> I am silver and exact. I have no preconceptions.
> . . . .
> Now I am a lake. A woman bends over me,
> Searching my reaches for what she really is.
> Then she turns to those liars, the candles or the moon.
> I see her back, and reflect it faithfully.
> . . . .

Each morning it is her face that replaces the darkness.
In me she has drowned a young girl, and in me an old woman
Rises toward her day after day, like a terrible fish. (p. 34)

Related to the effacement imagery of water, and of whiteness and blankness, is the mythological allusion to Lethe, used so effectively in the late poems "Amnesiac" and "Getting There":

Planets pulse in the lake like bright amoebas;
The pines blot our voices up in their lightest sighs.

Around our tent the old simplicities sough
Sleepily as Lethe, trying to get in.
We'll wake blank-brained as water in the dawn.
                    ("Two Campers in Cloud Country")

Further, "Face-Lift," a poem in which the woman's face-lift operation sounds very much like suicide, shows clearly, and for the first time, the reincarnation image so common in *Ariel:* "Mother to myself, I wake swaddled in gauze,/ Pink and smooth as a baby." (p. 6)

And the saint-sinner conflict, so thematically central to the early poetry, is evident in this transitional work as well, but with a significant difference. Whereas in the *Colossus* poems Plath chose to express this split in separate, opposing poems (as in "Spinster" versus "Strumpet Song," for instance), she here expresses it within a single poem, "In Plaster":

I shall never get out of this! There are two of me now:
This new absolutely white person and the old yellow one,
And the white person is certainly the superior one.
She doesn't need food, she is one of the real saints.
. . . .
I used to think we might make a go of it together—
After all, it was a kind of marriage, being so close.
Now I see it must be one or the other of us.
She may be a saint, and I may be ugly and hairy,
But she'll soon find out that that doesn't matter a bit.
I'm collecting my strength; one day I shall manage without her,
And she'll perish with emptiness then, and begin to miss me.

This technique, of manifesting conflicting aspects of the self within a single speaker, certainly emphasizes the desperate, intense aspect of this split. And after experimenting with this technique in "In Plaster," Plath skillfully reemploys it in such late poems as "Lesbos" and "Fever 103°."

IV *Toward* Ariel

The poems of Sylvia Plath's transitional period, then, are developmentally significant in several ways. And in this light, even their failures are important, for they reveal the poet's continuing efforts to shape the materials of her craft to her special use, to find her own voice. Furthermore, it would be inaccurate to imply that there are not some very fine poems among them. In a few instances, Plath seems not to have been able to maintain the intellectual defenses which denied life and power to so many of these transitional poems, and she created instead the direct, affecting kind of poem which was to become the predominant mode of the final work.

One of these poems is "Private Ground." Outstanding for its skillful use of sound and rhythm, this poem reflects the change in oral quality from Plath's early to her late work; it catches the reader's attention in the cadences of the very first line: "First frost, and I walk among the rosefruit," (p. 21) and continues throughout to evince a very readable, and a spoken, texture.

Another fine poem in *Crossing the Water* is "Blackberrying." Belonging to the landscape tradition of such earlier poems as "Point Shirley" and "Watercolor of Grantchester Meadows" and of so many transitional poems, this work shows one direction in which Plath's verse was going:

> Nobody in the lane, and nothing, nothing but blackberries,
> Blackberries on either side, though on the right mainly,
> A blackberry alley, going down in hooks, and a sea
> Somewhere at the end of it, heaving.

The plain description of the external landscape in this poem is powerful and lively. But beyond that, rhythms and word sounds afford to the experience a distorted quality which suggests that this landscape is internal as well:

> Blackberries
> Big as the ball of my thumb, and dumb as eyes
> Ebon in the hedges, fat

With blue-red juices. These they squander on my fingers.
I had not asked for such a blood sisterhood; they must love me.
They accommodate themselves to my milkbottle,
    flattening their sides.

"The Surgeon at 2 A.M." shows a similar, and more pronounced, external-internal distortion. Performing his operation in a white, sterile environment, the surgeon describes a procedure which belongs more to the nightmare (appropriately, the time is 2:00 A.M.) than to the operating room:

> The white light is artificial, and hygienic as heaven.
> The microbes cannot survive it.
> They are departing in their transparent garments, turned aside
> From the scalpels and the rubber hands.
> The scalded sheet is now a snowfield, frozen and peaceful.
> The body under it is in my hands.
> As usual there is no face. A lump of Chinese white
> With seven holes thumbed in.

Notice, too, the imagery of white, cold, and freezing, of flowers, color, and blooming, of hooks (specifically used in "Blackberrying" as well), and of perfection, so familiar in the later poems:

> It is a garden I have to do with—tubers and fruits
> Oozing their jammy substances,
> A mat of roots. My assistants hook them back.
> Stenches and colours assail me.
> This is the lung-tree.
> These orchids are splendid. They spot and coil like snakes.
> The heart is a red-bell-bloom, in distress.
> . . . .
>
> The blood is a sunset. I admire it.
> I am up to my elbows in it, red and squeaking,
> Still it seeps up, it is not exhausted.
> So magical! A hot spring
> I must seal off and let fill
> The intricate, blue piping under this pale marble.
> . . . .
>
> It is a statue the orderlies are wheeling off.
> I have perfected it.

In the speaker's cool, bizarre fascination with fantastic, horrible events, this poem is as excellent as any in the *Ariel* collection.

Not quite as fine, but well worth mention, is another poem from this transitional period. This one, "Widow," poignantly records the feelings of rejection, deep loneliness, and loss which may have reflected Sylvia Plath's own feelings at the time about her failing marriage. Though the poem suffers somewhat from the self-consciousness which enfeebles so much of this transitional work, it does generally succeed in presenting the drained voice and the bare confrontation with the void which are such compelling qualities in the late poetry.

In "Widow," a number of major motifs from the early poems are drawn together and treated with brutal honesty; problems with father, sex, love, despair, and frustration meld with the poet's intense energy and skill to produce, truly, "the first eruption of the voice that produced *Ariel*." The poem's first two stanzas, in a calm, almost exhausted mood, begin with these lines: "Widow. The word consumes itself—/. . ./Widow. The dead syllable, with its shadow/Of an echo. . . ." (p. 22) Intensity builds in stanzas three and four as the mood shifts gradually from numbness to animosity and the poet confuses husband with father:

> Widow. The bitter spider sits
> And sits in the center of her loveless spokes.
> Death is the dress she wears, her hat and collar.
> The moth-face of her husband, moonwhite and ill,
> Circles her like a prey she'd love to kill
>
> A second time, to have him near again—

And the intensity reaches its climax in stanza five:

> Widow: that great, vacant estate!
> The voice of God is full of draughtiness,
> Promising simply the hard stars, the space
> Of immortal blankness between stars

then begins to subside as animosity recedes: "Widow, the compassionate trees bend in, The trees of loneliness, the trees of mourning." (p. 23) The poem closes in relative calm as the poet expresses her sense of helpless isolation:

A bodiless soul could pass another soul
In this clear air and never notice it—
One soul pass through the other, frail as smoke
And utterly ignorant of the way it tool.

This is the fear she has—the fear
His soul may beat and be beating at her dull sense
Like blue Mary's angel, dovelike against a pane
Blinded to all but the grey, spiritless room
It looks in on, and must go on looking in on.

Thematically, two late poems join well with "Widow" to pose the poet's general dilemma as she expresses it in the work of the transitional period. "Amnesiac" is one of these, in its expression of the poet's isolation and the ambivalence of wife toward husband. The poem opens with:

No use, no use, now begging Recognize!
There is nothing to do with such a beautiful blank but smooth it.
Name, house, car keys,

The little toy wife—
Erased, sigh, sigh.

The sexual conflicts, so compellingly expressed in the early poems in terms of classical reference, are now clearly expanded to include husband as well as father:

Hugging his pillow

Like the red-haired sister he never dared to touch,
He dreams of a new one—
Barren, the lot are barren!

And for the first time, the conclusion points in that inevitable direction, anticipating the Lethe of "Getting There": "O sister, mother, wife,/Sweet Lethe is my life./I am never, never, never coming home!"[16]

In its beseeching tone and its desperate hope that all may not be lost, "Mystic" also belongs more to the transitional than the late work. Yet at the same time, as it discards, one by one, possible sources of meaning, of spiritual or emotional sustenance, it belongs firmly in the late period, where hope is abandoned:

Once one has seen God, what is the remedy?
Once one has been seized up

Without a part left over—
. . . .

What is the remedy?

The pill of the Communion tablet,
The walking beside still water? Memory?
. . . .

Is there no great love, only tenderness?
Does the sea

Remember the walker upon it?[17]

The special combination of desperation and restraint, of power and control so striking in the final poems is evident here—not only in "Mystic" and "Amnesiac," but in the transitional "Widow" as well.

Yet the poems of this transitional period are relatively subdued compared with those in *Ariel* and *Winter Trees;* subdued, in fact, because of their special, and necessary, transitional aspect. In the poems of *Crossing the Water,* Sylvia Plath's technique is in the process of becoming, of developing from an experimental to a finely honed and natural mode. It is in the transitional work that the change in oral quality occurs, so that we see, in the individual poems of this period, the shift in Plath's verse from a written to a spoken language. Moreover, the poet's extreme self-consciousness, responsible for the mediocrity of so many of these transitional poems, is perhaps a necessary qualification for the precision of the late work; here, the poet comes to know herself, so that her attitudes can be expressed, rather than explained, in her final poetry.

For there, in the poems of *Winter Trees* and *Ariel,* there is little search for new meaning and no self-pity whatever. The writing in the late poems exudes a sense of feverish necessity whose motivation is, as Stephen Spender observes, "pure need of expression."[18] Indeed, Sylvia Plath herself announces there that "The blood jet is poetry,/There is no stopping it."[19]

CHAPTER 5

Late Poetry

COLLECTED in the posthumous volumes *Ariel* and *Winter Trees*, most of these poems belong to the last year of the poet's life, a period bounded by the birth of her son Nicholas in January, 1962, and her suicide in February, 1963. That year was a time both of great personal upheaval and great creative productivity for Plath. After her husband left her in the summer of 1962, she lived for a time alone with her two children in their Devon home before moving, in December, to London to seek a new life. Her health was poor; both in Devon and in London, she fought the combined hardships of flu and high fever, and cold, damp weather. Yet she wrote more urgently than ever before; she daily set aside the very early morning hours for her poetry, composing, as she said, "a poem a day before breakfast."

The principal characteristic of Plath's late poems, and what distinguishes them from the poems of her transitional period, is their innate intensity combined with their ease of composition. In this late work, composed so rapidly, Plath had indeed found her own voice, or as Ted Hughes observes in "The Chronological Order of Sylvia Plath's Poems," "she had arrived . . . at her own centre of gravity." Abandoning her customary method of working slowly and laboriously to compose her poems, with a thesaurus close at hand, Plath now wrote "at top speed, as one might write an urgent letter."[1] All of the poems which Plath wrote in the last year of her life were composed in this way. A few, written a bit earlier but in similar fashion, are also appropriately included in this late group.

With the help of Hughes's notes, we may specifically date the composition of most of the *Ariel* poems. What he calls "the final phase" begins in April, 1962, with the composition of "Elm" and "The Moon and the Yew Tree," both of which were inspired by the immediate surroundings of the Hughes' Devon home. "The Rival" was written soon after, followed by "Berck-Plage" in July, 1962, a poem which recalls the Hughes' visit in the summer of 1961 to the French seaside resort by that name. Another group belongs to October and November of 1962. The Bee poems were written first; these are "The Bee Meeting," "The Arrival of the Bee Box," "Stings," "Wintering," and "The Swarm" (a poem included in the British edition of *Winter Trees* and the American *Ariel*). Next followed seventeen poems: "The Couriers," "Sheep in Fog," "The Applicant," "Lady Lazarus," "Cut," "The Night Dances," "Poppies in October," "Ariel" (which was the name of the horse Plath rode in Devon), "Death & Co.," "Nick and the Candlestick" (after Nicholas, Plath's son), "Gulliver," "Getting There," "Medusa," "A Birthday Present," "Letter in November," "Daddy," and "Fever 103." A final group of poems was written in January, 1963, Plath's last month; first came "The Munich Mannequins," "Totem," and "Paralytic." Plath wrote five others—"Balloons," "Contusion," "Kindness," "Edge," and "Words"—in the final week of her life.

This accounts for thirty-five of the forty poems which appear in the British edition of *Ariel* (published in 1965). Hughes mentions four others, which properly belong to this late period but were composed somewhat earlier, before Plath's last year. One of these is "You're," written in early 1960, shortly after the Hugheses' return to England and shortly before the birth of their daughter Frieda in April; this poem, according to Hughes, followed shortly after the *Colossus* poem "The Stones," and belongs to "the first eruption of the voice that produced Ariel." That voice is heard also in three other poems actually written within the transitional year of 1961; these are "Tulips," "Morning Song," and "Little Fugue." The three poems which Hughes fails to mention—"The Hanging Man," "Poppies in July," and "Years"—clearly belong among the late poems, because of their subjects and styles.

Once again, in the manner of Plath's early and transitional volumes, the British and American versions of *Ariel* differ slightly. The American edition (1966) contains all forty of the poems which first appeared in the British edition, plus three additional ones: "Mary's Song, " "Lesbos," and "The Swarm." "The Swarm," as we have seen, belongs with the Bee poems of October, 1962. Both "Mary's Song" and "Lesbos" are important late poems; "Mary's Song" was first published in 1962, and "Lesbos" was published originally in 1963. All three of these works, which are included only in the American *Ariel*, appear in the British *Winter Trees*.

Winter Trees, the fourth published volume of Plath's poetry, appeared posthumously; the British edition was published and an American edition followed the next year. With the volume *Ariel*, *Winter Trees* represents the work of Plath's late period; indeed, as Ted Hughes has written in a prefatory note to the volume, these poems "are all out of the batch from which the *Ariel* poems were more or less arbitrarily chosen and they were all composed in the last year of Sylvia Plath's life."[2] This is a relatively slim volume; the British edition contains nineteen poems and the American, twenty-five. To be accurate, Plath did write at least one of the *Winter Trees* poems before her last year; the composition of "The Rabbit Catcher" is dated, in *Lyonnesse*, as 1961. And, as Hughes observes in his prefatory note, "Three Women: a Poem for Three Voices," written slightly earlier, "can be seen as a bridge between *The Colossus* and *Ariel*, both in the change of style . . . and in that it was written to be read aloud."[3]

We know that Plath wrote three of the *Winter Trees* poems in the last month of her life; *Lyonnesse* and *Crystal Gazer* designate the year 1963 for the composition of "Child," "Gigolo," and "Lyonnesse." These poems, together with the two earlier ones, appear in both editions of *Winter Trees*, as do the title poem, "Brasilia," "Childless Woman," "Purdah," "The Courage of Shutting-up," "The Other," "Stopped Dead," "Mystic," "By Candlelight," "Thalidomide," and "For a Fatherless Son." The three poems which complete the contents for the Faber *Winter Trees* are those ("Lesbos," "The Swarm," and "Mary's Song") which appear in the American *Ariel*. And the nine poems which complete the American *Winter Trees* are the six which appeared in the British but not the American *Crossing the Water* and which are, indeed, transitional poems ("Apprehensions," "An Appearance," "Among the Narcissi," "Event," "Pheasant," and "The Tour"), plus three poems which appear in no other commercial volume: "Eavesdropper," "The Detective," and "Amnesiac."

I *Fusions*

The world of these late poems is the world of a nightmare, though there are constant objects and places in it which define its boundaries, which allow the visitor to recognize its outlines, and which afford the poetry much of its control. This world is made up mostly of aspects of the several worlds of the early poetry, now assimilated and working together.

There are, as Stephen Spender notes, "the dark outlines of a mythology of people and places which provide the structure of the control, the landmarks among which the poetry is moving."[4] Not only do Orestes, Oedipus, and Lethe appear in this dark mythology; others such as Cerberus, Ariel, Medusa, and various biblical characters play their part. The poet's German father figures darkly and often in reference to persons and to concentration camps. A necessary gothic moon provides the light, and the yew tree stands blackly by. Permeating these dark landmarks is the wild seascape of the poet's childhood, its recollected feel and smell as well as the emotions associated with it. All these provide at once the reserve from which the poet draws her imagery and symbolism and the referents where meaning resides.

Indeed, Sylvia Plath herself offers valuable commentary concerning the means by which private experience and sensibility is made accessible and public in these late poems. As the poet commented in an interview conducted a year before her death:

I think my poems immediately come out of the sensuous and emotional experiences I have, but I must say I cannot sympathize with these cries from the heart that are informed by nothing except a needle or a knife. . . . I believe that one should be able to control and manipulate experiences, even the most terrifying, like madness, being tortured . . . , with an informed and intelligent mind. I think that personal experience is very important, but certainly it shouldn't be a . . . narcissistic experience. I believe it should be *relevant,* and relevant to the larger things, the bigger things such as Hiroshima and Dachau and so on.[5]

Thus, to adopt Plath's chosen example, a "relevant" issue like Dachau becomes in her poems an analogue for the private experience she presents. For one thing, Dachau is not merely an external, distant, politically interesting place for Plath; she admits that, because of her own paternal German and maternal Austrian origin, her "concern with concentration camps and so on is uniquely intense."[6] Already, then, external-internal perimeters are being shifted; the poet's interest in Dachau is simultaneously personal and objective. And once this link between the inner and outer world is established, analogy can become metaphor. Father can become Nazi, with all of the rigidity and suppression and atrocity suggested thereby; daughter, becoming a Jewish victim, has found the natural vehicle to express her feelings of helplessness, rage, bitterness, and so forth.

In Sylvia Plath's late poems, the ultimate result of this linking of the inner with the outer world is that distinctions between external and internal reality are virtually removed. Landscape exists only as the poet perceives it. In Spender's words, "the landscape is an entirely interior, mental one in which external objects have become converted into symbols of hysterical vision." Nature is as much inside the poet as it is outside of her, or "if there are some externals in these poems . . . they exist in an atmosphere where the external is in immediate process of becoming the internal, opposites identical with one another."[7] "Getting There" serves as a good example of such internal-external fusion:

> The gigantic gorilla interior
> Of the wheels move, they appal me—
> The terrible brains
> Of Krupp, black muzzles
> Revolving, the sound
> Punching out Absence! Like cannon.
> . . . .
>
> There is mud on my feet,
> Thick, red and slipping, It is Adam's side,
> This earth I rise from, and I in agony.
> I cannot undo myself, and the train is steaming.
> Steaming and breathing, its teeth
> Ready to roll, like a devil's.
> . . . .
>
> It is so small
> The place I am getting to, why are there these obstacles—
> . . . .
>
> The fire's between us.
> Is there no still place
> Turning and turning in the middle air,
> Untouched and untouchable.
> The train is dragging itself, it is screaming—
> An animal
> Insane for the destination,
> The bloodspot,
> The face at the end of the flare.[8]

The common ground on which external and internal meet and merge in this poem is the notion of rushing—of rushing toward an established, anticipated goal. In terms of external reality, the forward momentum belongs to the train, carrying Nazi victims, rushing through the countryside toward its next, or last, stop—possibly a concentration camp. In terms of internal reality, the forward momentum belongs to a person, one of the train's passengers and thus a victim, rushing also toward a known terminal. The nature and quality of this journey is defined by the surreal merging of inner and outer realities. The train's interior and wheels are "appalling" (note the pun); the vehicle is a gorilla, a devil with fangs, a screaming animal insane for the destination. In this nightmare world, the victim slides and slips in thick red mud, driven in forward motion, helpless to disembark.

Death is "the place" this passenger is "getting to," the "still place" in most of these poems. It is part of Plath's special landscape and is omnipresent in her set of particularized images, where internal and external realities blend so completely that one becomes indistinguishable from the other. As A. R. Jones aptly observes, "the relationship between the inner and outer worlds is fractured, the outer world holding up a mirror in which the inner world can see its distorted self."[9] We see an interesting correlate to this process, especially in light of "Getting There," in *The Bell Jar*, where Esther Greenwood is describing a skiing experience: "I plummeted down past the zigzaggers, the students, the experts, through year after year of doubleness and smiles and compromise, into my own past. People and trees receded on either hand like the dark sides of a tunnel as I hurtled on to the still, bright point at the end of it, the pebble at the bottom of the well, the white sweet baby cradled in its mother's belly" (*B*, 108). Whether the destination is expressed in terms of still points, of dewdrops, of bloodspots, of new babies, or of submerged rocks, in nearly all of the late poems, the poet is indeed "getting there."

Much of this death imagery seems to grow from Plath's recollections of her sea childhood. In "Ocean 1212-W" she recalls how she could never watch her "grandmother drop the dark green lobsters . . . into the boiling pot from which they would be, in a minute, drawn—red, dead, and edible. I felt the awful scald of the water too keenly on my skin." (p. 313). Death is red in "Getting There," as it is in easily one half of the poems in *Ariel* and *Winter Trees:*

> I am red meat.
> . . . .
>
> I do not stir.
>
>
> The dead bell,
> The dead bell.
>
> Somebody's done for. ("Death & Co.")

And often death is both red and scalding:

> And I
> Am the arrow,
>
> The dew that flies
> Suicidal, at one with the drive
> Into the red
>
> Eye, the cauldron of morning. ("Ariel")

Death is also a glitter in these poems. In "Berck-Plage" where
"An old man is vanishing," "things are glittering." In "Gigolo," the
speaker "glitter[s] like Fontainebleau,"[10] and the undertaker in
"Death & Co." is a "Bastard/Masturbating a glitter." Mirrors glitter
too, and mirrors represent death in many of the poems; in "The
Courage of Shutting-Up," for example, mirrors "can kill," and in
"Contusion" "the mirrors are sheeted" after "the heart shuts." Glitter goes also with the sea in Plath's association, and sea is death as
well: "Even with my eyes shut I could feel the glimmers of [the
sea's] bright mirrors spider over my lids." Her childhood sea was
"like a deep woman, it hid a good deal; it had many faces, many
delicate, terrible veils. It spoke of miracles and distances; if it could
court, it could also kill." She can remember crawling into it, fascinated, before she could walk, nearly drowning.[11] And these associations become images in the late poems, for example in "A Birthday
Present":

> What is this, behind this veil, is it ugly, is it beautiful?
> Is it shimmering, has it breasts, has it edges?
> . . . .

But it shimmers, it does not stop, and I think it wants me.
. . . .

Only let down the veil, the veil, the veil.
If it were death

I would admire the deep gravity of it, its timeless eyes.

The landscape is a deathly landscape, then; such things as the landmarks and objects in "Getting There" and the elements of the seascape are at once objective and subjective items and conditions. Even common household objects become internalized and strange under the distorted, surreal gaze of the poet:

Viciousness in the kitchen!
The potatoes hiss,
It is all Hollywood, windowless,
The fluorescent light wincing on and off like a terrible migraine

Coy paper strips for doors—
Stage curtains, a widow's frizz. ("Lesbos")

This fusion of external and internal landscape seems, in its particular manifestations, a kind of weird, updated metaphysical conceit. Nor is this the only kind of fusion of opposites in these late poems; the opposites of love and hate are fused as well, with death as the catalyst. Even in death there is a merging of opposites, for death is both the act of loving, the lover, and the only possible place to find love. Clearly, Plath has achieved excellence in the late works through her controlled and organic manipulation of imagery. Indeed, in a number of the *Ariel* and *Winter Trees* poems, the progressive linking of one image to the next creates a new order of reality for the whole poem in much the same way that the creating of a single metaphor makes us see differently, or more clearly.

The form of "Little Fugue," for example, is determined by the musical structure for which the poem is named. Subject and countersubject are introduced in the first stanza:

The yew's black fingers wag;
Cold clouds go over.
So the deaf and dumb
Signal the blind, and are ignored.

and the subject is repeated through the poem in three more
" "voices" ": "A yew hedge of orders . . ."; "The yew my Christ,
then . . ."; "And you, during the Great War . . ."; so that by the
time the development is ended, the black yew stands for senseless,
"deaf and dumb" tyranny and oppression in its manifestations of
death, Nazi father, and Christ's executioners; and the countersubject, the white cloud, stands for the innocent "blind" victim, in its
manifestations of featurelessness, emptiness, and pallor.

A closer study of another poem, "Mary's Song," reveals specifically how this linking of images works. The Mary of this excellent
poem is at once Christ's mother and the poet herself, and sacrifice is
the general concept which controls specific images:

> The Sunday lamb cracks in its fat.
> The fat
> Sacrifices its opacity. . . .
>
> A window, holy gold.
> The fire makes it precious,
> The same fire
>
> Melting the tallow heretics,
> Ousting the Jews.
> Their thick palls float
>
> Over the cicatrix of Poland, burnt-out
> Germany.
> They do not die.
>
> Grey birds obsess my heart,
> Mouth-ash, ash of eye.
> They settle. On the high
>
> Precipice
> That emptied one man into space
> The ovens glowed like heavens, incandescent.
>
> It is a heart,
> This holocaust I walk in,
> O golden child the world will kill and eat.

The "Sunday lamb" cooking for dinner is also Christ, the sacrificial
Lamb. As this lamb cooks, the fat on the outside of it "sacrifices its

opacity," becoming crispy and golden—thereby "precious." And the same fire which kills and cooks the lamb (or the Lamb), melts his fat, and makes him precious through sacrifice, also kills the Jews (Christ was a Jew) and melts their "tallow." So that the smoke and ashes (note the several meanings of "palls") of their sacrifice can float over Germany, the home of the victimizers, suggesting a kind of resurrection which maintains the Christ parallel. Ashes from these sacrifices, as they float, settle on Mary, the survivor, reminding her of both the crucifixion and the Nazi ovens; her world is now both ashen grey and a "holocaust." And the poem's last line points in a new direction; the world has killed the lamb, the "golden child," but the process of eating it (Him) suggests the sacrament of communion.

Certainly, the ordering and juxtaposing of images in this poem creates richly a new kind of reality. The motif of the Jew as Nazi victim belongs to the poet's personal symbology, and we remember her constant use of this image to describe herself and her condition. Her linking of this Jewish victim with Christ and with her own baby boy is this poem, and her female connection of all three victims with a roasting lamb, certainly creates for the reader a new way of seeing each and all of these elements.

II *Conflicts*

The strumpet-spinster conflict of the early poems and of the transitional poem "In Plaster" is powerfully expressed in these late ones, usually in a kind of schizoid manner within a single poem. In "The Other," for instance, "I" and "you" are irrevocably sundered; "I," the speaker, exclaims: "Cold glass, how you insert yourself/ Between myself and myself./ I scratch like a cat." And in "Lesbos," strumpet and spinster assume separate identities. The device of the double which we have observed elsewhere in Plath's work, most notably in *The Bell Jar*, works here, as we hear a woman talking to herself. "I," the speaker, is strumpet: "I should sit on a rock off Cornwall and comb my hair./ I should wear tiger pants, I should have an affair." Yet we hear, in these "Prufrock"-like lines, a conflict even within the strumpet's consciousness. "You," the silent member of the conversation, is spinster: "You peer from the door,/ Sad hag. 'Every woman's a whore./ I can't communicate.' " The breakdown of communication is irrevocable and destructive: "I call you Orphan, orphan. You are ill./ . . . / I say I may be back./ You know what lies are for." This divided woman also has a child. And in

the forecast of suffering which results by extension for her baby, we
recognize also the effect of this inner conflict on the mother:

> And I, love, am a pathological liar,
> And my child—look at her, face down on the floor,
> Little unstrung puppet, kicking to disappear—
> Why she is schizophrenic,
> . . . .
> She'll cut her throat at ten if she's mad at two.

In other poems, the split selves of spinster and strumpet are
represented not as separate people, but as separate, vying forces.
"O love, O celibate," cries the speaker of "Letter in November."
The conflict may be realized in a number of ways—in the poem's
words directly, or in a close relation between the poem's sound and
sense, or in the poem's imagery. It may be expressed even in puns;
the speaker-victim of "Daddy" has chosen a husband with "a love of
the rack and the screw."

But no matter how it is rendered, the conflict involves the love
and hate of strumpet and celibate for one another, for their acts, and
for their chosen types of lovers. In its absolute impossibility of rec-
onciliation in life, the frustration requires death for its resolution, a
death which is at once actual and sexual, an end and a beginning.
And this inevitable death is not only accepted by the poet—it is
desired. As the conflict joins love with hate and end with beginning,
it also joins love with death. In "The Couriers," many familiar images connote death, while the poet speaks its conjunction with love:

> Frost on a leaf, the immaculate
> Cauldron, talking and crackling
> . . . .
>
> A disturbance in mirrors,
> The sea shattering its grey one—
>
> Love, love, my season.

The tension between all of these forces, desires, and restraints is
powerfully and excellently expressed in "Fever 103°." Here the
speaker's words express her inner conflict; though she has been in
bed with her lover all night, the strumpet has achieved only limited

success: "Darling, all night/ I have been flickering, off, on, off, on./
The sheets grow heavy as a lecher's kiss" and the spinster, who has
been asking disturbing questions about purity, punishment, and
adultery, has finally gained control: "I am too pure for you or anyone./ Your body/ Hurts me as the world hurts God. I am a lan-
tern—" But the control is of the mind only. Her new heat and
passion are, in the words' meaning, the heat of religious fervor, of an
"acetylene Virgin." But the poem's rhythms say that her heat and
passion are intensely sexual; as the lines decrease in length, as the
cadences become regular and then grow rhythmically faster and
shorter, what we hear, not in words, is an incredible build toward
orgasm:

> Does not my heat astound you. And my light.
> All by myself I am a huge camellia
> Glowing and coming and going, flush on flush.
>
> I think I am going up,
> I think I may rise—
> The beads of hot metal fly, and I, love, I
>
> Am a pure acetylene
> Virgin
> Attended by roses,
>
> By kisses, by cherubim,
> By whatever these pink things mean.
> Not you, nor him
>
> Not him, nor him
> (My selves dissolving, old whore petticoats)—
> To Paradise.

an orgasm which insists on the conflict by denying its very existence
at the climactic moment ("Virgin"), and which is at once sexual
release, and a release into death.

The conflict is complex and unresolvable. The despair which it
engendered in the earlier poems has now changed to resignation,
expressed in various moods. The desperate hope of "Mystic" is
largely absent from the final poems, and when the poet is not
loudly, or mockingly, or defiantly decrying her fate, she is describing it in an empty, flat voice:

> This is the light of the mind, cold and planetary.
> . . . .
>
> The moon is no door. It is a face in its own right,
> . . . .
>
> With the O-gape of complete despair. I live here.
> . . . .
>
> The yew tree points up. It has a Gothic shape.
> The eyes lift after it and find the moon.
> The moon is my mother. She is not sweet Mary.
> Her blue garments unloose small bats and owls.
> How I would like to believe in tenderness—
> . . . .
>
> The moon sees nothing of this. She is bald and wild.
> And the message of the yew tree is blackness—blackness and
> silence. ("The Moon and the Yew Tree")

In spite of such generally prevalent blankness and despair in these late poems, however, there are among them several "baby" poems, addressed lovingly by the speaker to her child. For brief moments, perhaps, the mother's love may provide partial relief from the otherwise unrelieved world of nightmare. "You're" is an affectionate, droll poem, with wonderfully clever images. There, the baby is

> Clownlike, happiest on your hands,
> . . . .
> Mute as a turnip from the Fourth
> Of July to All Fool's Day.
> O high-riser, my little loaf.
>
> . . . .
> Jumpy as a Mexican bean.
> Right, like a well-done sum.
> A clean slate, with your own face on.

The child is innocent, new, unacquainted with pain; in "Child," similarly, his "clear eye is the one absolutely beautiful thing./ I want to fill it with colour and ducks." Too, "Morning Song" and "Balloons" and "For a Fatherless Son" are loving and whimsical musings of mother to baby. In these poems the child's "clear vowels rise like balloons"; he is a precious little bundle of time, a "fat gold watch" recently "set going" by "Love"; his "smiles are found money."

Yet the imagery of disintegration and death invades even these poems. The baby of "You're" is "moon-skulled"; in "Child" he

> Should be grand and classical
>
> Not this troublous
> Wringing of hands, this dark
> Ceiling without a star.

The precious child of "Morning Song" is also a "New statue/ In a drafty museum"; in "Balloons" he holds "a red/ Shred in his little fist"; and the fatherless son "will be aware of an absence, presently,/ Growing beside you like a tree,/ A death tree, colour gone." There are dead babies in "Death & Co.," and the woman who is perfected by death in "Edge" holds her dead children at her breast.

And so the unmitigated conflict, "this dark thing" of "Elm," unbearably rages and bursts out in a single cry:

> I am inhabited by a cry.
> Nightly it flaps out
> Looking, with its hooks, for something to love.
>
> I am terrified by this dark thing
> That sleeps in me;
> . . . .
>
> What is this, this face
> So murderous in its strangle of branches—?
>
> Its snaky acids kiss.
> It petrifies the will. These are the isolate, slow faults
> That kill, that kill, that kill.

III   *Formal Control*

There is no letting up in these poems, no release whatever. The poet is indeed inhabited by her cry; her nightmare is real, and reality is the nightmare. And in informing it, much of the power derives from the controlling, but not taming, influence the poetic structure exerts upon the poet's outpourings. Not only do the breakdown of exterior-interior boundaries, the highly symbolic landscape, and the particularized set of images require special control because of their wild, hallucinatory nature; they also, at the same time, provide control as they define the limits of a nightmarish world. In this poetry, well-established boundaries guide the turbulent stream and cause it to flow faster. Economy relates directly to intensity.

In this economizing, intensifying role, the poems' structures play an important part. Most of the poems in *Ariel* and *Winter Trees* differ from the earlier ones, as we have seen, by being more emphatic, more direct, simpler, and more linguistically natural. And the increase in excellence here is related in part to a decreasing concern on Sylvia Plath's part with formal stanza and end-rhyme constructions.

One exception to this rule, however, demands attention. The only poem among the late ones with consistent end-rhyme and rhythmic regularity from beginning to end is "Daddy," a poem which suffers no loss of power from its apparently conventional structure. Its rhythm is anapestic trimeter with many irregularities; its end-rhyme, "oo," falls into no particular pattern but concludes a minimum of one line in every five-line stanza (with the exception of only one stanza out of sixteen where it is not used at all) and a maximum of five lines. In these sounds and rhythms, "Daddy" has clear affinities with the nursery rhyme, a mode which provides, in this case, an obviously ironic structure. Indeed, in her adoption of this form, Plath has intentionally linked the nursery-rhyme world with the world of the poem to create a precariously balanced tension between the two. Further, as A. Alvarez suggests, the nursery rhyme may have provided for Plath an essential "manic defence" against the insufferable.[12] Certainly, this is Plath's starkest confrontation with the "daddy" problem evident throughout her work; since the sense which drives this poem is perhaps more painful to her than any other, a real need may exist for the extra edge of control afforded by regular form. The rhythm is the rhythm of ritual, and the ritual is one both of death and of love. A. R. Jones observes that the poem's "main area of conflict" is the psyche of the persecuted speaker, with its final knowledge, from which she can escape only into death, that love expresses itself only in terms of violence and brutality.[13]

In spite of the regularity, then, this poem is not a misfit in *Ariel;*

the form is anything but rigid, and the poem reveals the same line to line power seen in all of the other late poems. The "Daddy" of the poem is the colossus; here he is both daddy and husband. And the work jauntily but terrifyingly synthesizes the poet's problem:

> You do not do, you do not do
> Any more, black shoe
> In which I have lived like a foot
> For thirty years, poor and white,
> Barely daring to breathe or Achoo.
> . . . .
>
> I was ten when they buried you.
> At twenty I tried to die
> And get back, back, back to you.
> I thought even the bones would do.
>
> But they pulled me out of the sack,
> And they stuck me together with glue.
> And then I know what to do.
> I made a model of you,
> A man in black with a Meinkampf look
>
> And a love of the rack and the screw.
> And I said I do, I do.
> So daddy, I'm finally through.
> The black telephone's off at the root,
> The voices just can't worm through.
>
> If I've killed one man, I've killed two—
> The vampire who said he was you
> And drank my blood for a year,
> Seven years, if you want to know.
> Daddy, you can lie back now.
>
> There's a stake in your fat black heart
> And the villagers never liked you.
> They are dancing and stamping on you.
> They always knew it was you.
> Daddy, daddy, you bastard, I'm through.

The other, less regular poems in *Ariel* and *Winter Trees* are powerful for basically the same reasons as "Daddy." Intensity resides in the emotion expressed, to be sure, but the poems are powerful because of the one-to-one relation between sense and structure. Aural texture is vivid and effective; Plath's experimentation with sound in the earlier works most certainly serves her well in these late ones. The tongue-twisting quality of such early poems as "Snake-charmer," "Sow," and "The Hermit at Outermost House" gives way, in the final poems, to the hightly appropriate sound patterns of such poems as "Daddy," or "Gigolo":

> Pocket watch, I tick well.
> The streets are lizardy crevices
> Sheer-sided, with holes where to hide.
> . . . .
>
> Bright fish hooks, the smiles of women
> Gulp at my bulk
> And I, in my snazzy blacks
>
> Mill a litter of breasts like jellyfish.
> To nourish
> The cellos of moans I eat eggs—

Here, word sounds reinforce one another to intensify meaning; indeed, word sounds actually *provide* meaning, so that the texture of the poem's language itself presents the experience being offered simultaneously in the poem.

Even more striking than the sounds of individual words is the feeling and even the sound of motion which the poetry projects through its line lengths and its distinct, though often fragmentary rhythms. Again, the poet's earlier experimentation with such stylized and demanding structures as the villanelle and terza rima, her practice in writing strictly patterned stanzas both long and short, serve her well in this late work. For the poems of *Ariel* and *Winter Trees* conform not to an externally imposed pattern, but rather to the pattern demanded by the poem's sense. Short lines, abrupt enjambements, and jerking rhythms effectively convey the speaker's clipped tones, laden with emotion and/or rage about to break the lines' tight restrictions, in such poems as "Lady Lazarus" or "Purdah":

> Attendants!
> And at his next step
> I shall unloose

> I shall unloose—
> From the small jewelled
> Doll he guards like a heart—
>
> The lioness,
> The shriek in the bath,
> The cloak of holes.   ("Purdah")

91-93

Longer lines, and easier rhythms, evoke also the speaker's emotional condition, whether it be the drained cadences of a poem like "Contusion":

> Colour floods to the spot, dull purple.
> The rest of the body is all washed out,
> The colour of pearl.
> . . . .
>
> The heart shuts,
> The sea slides back,
> The mirrors are sheeted.

or the wistful, poignant expression of the mother-to-child poems. In any case, rhythms, and line and stanza length (and, indeed, the length of the poem itself) are determined by sense; in the late poetry, structure and sense are joined inextricably. As Stephen Spender has commented, these poems are "outpouring[s] which could only stop with the lapsing of the poet's hysteria; . . . the length of the poem is decided by the duration of the poet's vision, which is far more serious to the poet than formal considerations."[14]

Closely connected, of course, to this organic relation of sense with structure is the oral quality achieved in the late poems. They require, as Sylvia Plath has remarked, to be read aloud. However various the cadences of *Ariel* and *Winter Trees* may be, they are the cadences of speech, the rhythms of a person talking. The poet has progressed from the often stilted rhythms of the early work, through the easier, more natural rhythms of *Crossing the Water*, to the appropriate and diverse rhythms of the last poems.

The voice play "Three Women" presents a fine example of this achievement. This "Poem for Three Voices" consists of a kind of triple dramatic monologue, offering in time sequence the experiences of three women before, during, and after miscarriage or childbirth. As such, it evinces not only Plath's achievement of veri-

similitude in her characters' speech, but also her shedding of the
self-consciousness so apparent in the transitional work, so that she
creates here believable, and forceful, dramatic situations.

The speakers of this dramatic voice poem are a wife, a secretary
(also a wife), and an unmarried girl. The setting, as Plath directs, is
"A Maternity Ward and round about." As the poem progresses,
each character recollects the series of events which brought her
there, and each, expressing her anticipations, fears, and thoughts, is
clearly individual and compellingly credible. For example, the
poem opens as the first voice (the wife) reflects upon her gravid
condition:

> When I walk out, I am a great event.
> I do not have to think, or even rehearse.
> What happens in me will happen without attention.
> The pheasant stands on the hill;
> He is arranging his brown feathers.
> I cannot help smiling at what it is I know.
> Leaves and petals attend me. I am ready.

The second voice (the secretary) has miscarried her baby; she describes her reaction in terms which echo another of Plath's late
poems, "The Moon and the Yew Tree":

> There is the moon in the high window. It is over.
> How winter fills my soul! And that chalk light
> Laying its scales on the windows, the windows of empty offices,
> Empty schoolrooms, empty churches. O so much emptiness!
> There is this cessation. This terrible cessation of everything.
> These bodies mounded around me now, these polar sleepers—
> What blue, moony ray ices their dreams?

And the third voice (the girl) expresses her fear before giving birth:

> And what if two lives leaked between my thighs?
> I have seen the white clean chamber with its instruments.
> It is a place of shrieks. It is not happy.
> "This is where you will come when you are ready."
> The night lights are flat red moons. They are dull with blood.
> I am not ready for anything to happen.
> I should have murdered this, that murders me.

As all three women speak, their voices are distinct and their diction appropriate. Only the first voice, as we come to know it, could express the mature calm of "I am ready"; only the second voice could utter the sharp despair of "I am restless. Restless and useless. I, too, create corpses." And only the girlish third voice, "not ready for anything to happen," could pronounce the second thought "I should have murdered this, that murders me." As Douglas Cleverdon observes, "the emotional experience" of the three women "is shaped by poetic discipline into the most austere and monosyllabic forms. In radio, nothing can equal a poet's visualizing imagination, dramatically expressed in clear and speakable language."[15] And, in fact, nothing can equal such an achievement in poetry, either.

IV Final Achievement

Clearly, then, Sylvia Plath's uses of sound and structure, of rhythm and language, are imaginative, varied, and always appropriate in her final poems; the lines which have been quoted from these poems attest to this and to the control and economy achieved thereby. The poet has truly become a master of her form; the poems now are economical and appropriate in technique, powerful and yet controlled in expression, and incisive and original in conception. Two final, specific examples will underline the point.

The poem "Tulips" exemplifies one particular style Plath uses; its lines are long and relatively smooth, and its rhythm is fairly constant though not conventionally regular. Its stanzas are like paragraphs, each one exploring a new area of the main idea. And each "paragraph" is unified by a single image which relates to every other unifying image all of which, together, comprise the whole poetic statement. The poem moves by means of its subtly shifting images as several aspects of a single scene are called to attention. The effect is that of a very simple red and white kaleidoscope; the scene's components obtrude and recede, and the pattern changes as values are transferred from one object to another. The "I" of the poem is a postoperative patient still in the hospital, "learning peacefulness, lying by myself quietly/ As the light lies on these white walls, . . ./ I am nobody." Quietness is the mood of sense and rhythm with a few notable exceptions. Stanza two presents an eye image:

> They have propped my head between the pillow and the sheet-cuff
> Like an eye between two white lids that will not shut.
> Stupid pupil, it has to take everything in.

"Stupid pupil" in the midst of longer, smoother phrases offers significant, thematic contrast. And the manipulation of imagery is particularly evident if we compare stanza 2 with stanza 7, where the pupil, the patient's white, "cut-paper shadow" non-face, now lies between red borders instead of white, themselves eyes:

> Nobody watched me before, now I am watched.
> The tulips turn to me, and the window behind me
> Where once a day the light slowly widens and slowly thins,
> And I see myself, flat, ridiculous, a cut-paper shadow
> Between the eye of the sun and the eyes of the tulips.
> And I have no face, I have wanted to efface myself.
> The vivid tulips eat my oxygen.

The last line of this stanza introduces the red and white air imagery of the next stanza, and so forth. Notice, too, the similarity of the "cut-paper shadow" here to the "cut-paper people" of the transitional poem "Crossing the Water." Surely the contrast between the effectiveness of that image in "Tulips" and its impotency in the earlier poem is one more positive testament to Plath's poetic achievement in her final work.

"Tulips" moves by subjective association, like a dream, or a nightmare. But the poet never releases her control, whether writing in the "tulips" style or in the jagged style she employs more often in *Ariel* and *Winter Trees*. Of this latter technique, the poem "Lady Lazarus" offers a particularly vivid example. The sense of a nightmarish circus world found in the early poem "Circus in Three Rings" pervades "Lady Lazarus," but the greater intensity of the later poem derives from the shorter, choppy lines, the overlay of a biting, sardonic tone onto the defiant mood, and the shifting rhythmic patterns. The speaker is the poet herself, "the magician's girl who does not flinch" ("the Bee Meeting"), a sort of circus freak lady. She begins:

> I have done it again.
> One year in every ten
> I manage it—
>
> A sort of walking miracle,
> . . . .

Peel off the napkin
O my enemy.
Do I terrify?—

The nose, the eye pits, the full set of teeth?
The sour breath
Will vanish in a day.
. . . .

What a million filaments.
The peanut-crunching crowd
Shoves in to see

Them unwrap me hand and foot—
The big strip tease.
Gentlemen, ladies,

These are my hands
My knees.
I may be skin and bone,

Nevertheless, I am the same, identical woman.

The poem jerks ahead through Lady Lazarus' hideous performance
as the calloused circus performer makes her bitterly trenchant
statement. And in determining the implications of that statement, a
look at the Lazarus reference is instructive. One biblical Lazarus,
the one we probably think of first in connection with Plath's poem,
is the one who was raised from the dead, emerging from his grave,
like the lady of the poem, "bound hand and foot with graveclothes:
and his face was bound about with a napkin" (John 11:44). Notice
how closely Plath uses the language of the biblical account. But
there is another Lazarus as well, a beggar, "full of sores" which "the
dogs came and licked." This beggar, Lazarus, is refused aid by a rich
man, and when both men die, it is Lazarus, and not the rich man,
who achieves heaven: "Remember," God says to the rich man, "that
thou in thy lifetime receivedst thy good things, and likewise Lazarus
evil things; but now he is comforted, and thou art tormented" (Luke
16:19–26). Beneath the defiant cadences of the poem, then, is both a
plea for help and a damning indictment of the unwilling helper.
Such a reading is certainly reinforced by the poem's familiar imagery of Jew and enemy. If Lady Lazarus—the poet herself, the

Jew—is in torment now, her victimizers will suffer great torment later. As the poem continues, its rhythm suddenly becomes quite regular as Lady Lazarus shifts into a bitter mocking of her "act" and even of herself:

> Dying
> Is an art, like everything else.
> I do it exceptionally well.
>
> I do it so it feels like hell.
> I do it so it feels real.
> I guess you could say I've a call.

Then, from this point to the poem's close, the two rhythms interchange and mingle.

No further testament is needed to the power of this poetry or the skill of its author. Sylvia Plath said once that the finest works of her favorite poets "seem born all-of-a-piece, not put together by hand";[16] in the late poems of *Ariel* and *Winter Trees*, she too has achieved this style. In her last years, Sylvia Plath disciplined her cry into a number of cogent, convincing poems in which all parts work perfectly together. She did indeed succeed in informing her "cries from the heart" and in ordering even the most terrifying of experiences; in this work, both poet and poem "melt to a shriek" which is at once utterly uncontrollable and finally controlled in the poem.

But does the fact of the poet's suicide finally negate the authenticity of the control which these poems place upon their turbulent subjects? Or, indeed, are those very subjects validated in some way by the poet's death? Robert Lowell concludes that these late poems of Sylvia Plath "tell that life, even when disciplined, is simply not worth it."[17] But that is only part of what they tell. For the poems themselves do live on, surviving the death of their composer, as in fact all poems do. As the poet Anne Sexton, a friend of Sylvia Plath's and herself a suicide, reminds us, "suicide is, after all, the opposite of the poem."[18] Finally, the poet's death must be regarded as an act which neither negates nor authenticates her work; death, after all, is not a poem. And these late poems, as Sylvia Plath herself observed when speaking of great poetry, go "farther than the words of a classroom teacher or the prescriptions of a doctor; if they are very lucky, farther than a lifetime."[19]

CHAPTER 6

God's Lioness

A S soon as the major techniques and concerns of this utterly
personal poetry emerge, one can see that it is essentially a
contemporary restatement of the apocalyptic vision. Decked with
surreal landscapes, mythological characters, scenes of World War II
horrors, and glimpses of modern domestic life, the essential vision
has been invoked and newly expressed to define the poet's present
misery and her anticipation of triumphant release.

Since the late poems represent a culmination, in their subjects,
images, and technical excellence, of Sylvia Plath's whole poetic
career, it is to these poems that we look for the most cogent statement of this vision. And in the same way that these final poems
contain the major concerns of the whole canon (remember Ted
Hughes' observation of "how faithfully her separate poems build up
into one long poem"), the title poem of the volume *Ariel* presents
the predominant concerns of the late work. "Ariel" is a compendium
of the poetry; in it we find the sense of present oppression and
despair, the belief in release from that oppression, and the notion of
relentlessly, uncontrollably speeding ahead through an antipathetic
landscape toward a goal which is at once destructive and ecstatic, an
end and a beginning.

On an obvious level, "Ariel" describes a dawn ride which begins
with the instant that the speaker, having mounted her horse, is
poised for action ("Stasis in darkness"), continues as she gathers
speed and intensity, and culminates as recognizable landscape dis-
solves and the speaker is violently propelled through air. Even in
the poem's opening lines we recognize that this ride will have intan-
gible as well as tangible qualities: "Stasis in darkness./ Then the
substanceless blue/ Pour of tor and distances."[1] Emerging from in-
action, perhaps even specifically from a dark stable, into the light of

97

early dawn, horse, rider, and landscape are all curiously "substanceless."

The effect of this "substanceless" quality is to permit a fusion of elements. Indeed, that fusion is the source both of the poem's strength and of its abstruseness; as A. Alvarez has pointed out, "the difficulty of this poem lies in separating one element from another. Yet that is also its theme; the rider is one with the horse, the horse is one with the furrowed earth, and the dew on the furrow is one with the rider."[2]

> God's lioness,
> How one we grow,
> Pivot of heels and knees!—The furrow
>
> Splits and passes, sister to
> The brown arc
> Of the neck I cannot catch,

In the "pivot of heels and knees," horse and rider visually become "one," and we are told that furrow and horse are sisters.

It is at this point that we recognize the poem's thematic center. The unity of rider with horse with furrow with dew, which Alvarez sees as the poem's theme, encompasses only a part of the poem's elements. At the center of this "substanceless" collection of ingredients is the word "Ariel." For one thing, Ariel is the name of Sylvia Plath's horse, and as Ted Hughes describes it, the experience which provides the simple, surface sense of the poem is an actual one: "Ariel was the name of the horse on which she went riding weekly. Long before, while she was a student at Cambridge (England), she went riding with an American friend out towards Grantchester. Her horse bolted, the stirrups fell off, and she came all the way home to the stables, about two miles, at full gallop, hanging around the horse's neck."[3] Included in this unity of elements, then, is not just any rider, but the poet herself. Parenthetically, it is interesting to note that "Ariel" is also the name of a kind of Arabian gazelle. It is entirely possible that Plath knew this, and chose for her horse's name one that suggested, among other things, the gazelle's swiftness.

The various Ariels from literature are also germane to the sense of this poem and of Plath's whole canon. Of principal importance is Shakespeare's Ariel, the tricksy spirit of *The Tempest*; since all things are fused in Plath's poem, since horse and earth and poet are one, then the spirit Ariel joins also in this unity. Several of his characteristics are relevant here; for one thing, he is the poet and singer who creates spells with his song. Furthermore, Shakespeare's Ariel, like the rebel angel of Milton's *Paradise Lost* and Belinda's guardian in Pope's *The Rape of the Lock*, is androgynous, capable of changing sex and shape at will. And so Plath, as Ariel, can be variously Lady Lazarus, an elm tree, a man applying for a wife, a mother, a Jew, a gigolo, and so forth. Finally, and perhaps most important, Shakespeare's Ariel is captive, held in servitude by his master Prospero:

> ARIEL: Is there more toil? Since thou dost give me pains,
> Let me remember thee what thou has promis'd,
> Which is not yet perform'd me.
> PROSPERO: How now! Moody?
> What is't thou canst demand?
> ARIEL: My liberty.
> PROSPERO: Before the time be out! No more! . . .
>   Thou shalt be as free
> As mountain winds; but then exactly do
> All points of my command.
> ARIEL: To the syllable.[4]

And significantly, one short poem in *Ariel*, "The Hanging Man," alludes directly to this Ariel of *The Tempest:*

> By the roots of my hair some god got hold of me.
> I sizzled in his blue volts like a desert prophet.
>
> The nights snapped out of sight like a lizard's eyelid:
> A world of bald white days in a shadeless socket.
>
> A vulturous boredom pinned me in this tree.
> If he were I, he would do what I did.[5]

This sense of present oppression and anticipation of release and freedom is thematically central to Sylvia Plath's poetry. It may be expressed, for example, as attainment of "perfection," as in "Edge," where the dead woman "is perfected," or in "The Munich Mannequins" ("Perfection is terrible, it cannot have children"), or in "Three Women," where the secretary's aborted fetus is

> the unborn one that loved its perfections,
> The face of the dead one that could only be perfect
> In its easy peace, could only keep holy so.[6]

Or it may appear as the queen bee's triumphant and phoenixlike flight from those who would retain and kill her, or as suicidal escape from the murderous influence of daddy and husband.

Moreover, this theme of oppression and release is invoked in yet another way, and the reference is ultimately significant not only to the poem "Ariel," but to Plath's entire vision. In "Purdah," the poet characterizes that part of herself which rages for release, which thirsts for destruction (and self-destruction), as a "lioness":

> I shall unloose—
> From the small jewelled
> Doll he guards like a heart—
>
> The lioness,
> The shriek in the bath,
> The cloak of holes.[7]

And in "Ariel," she becomes the lioness totally: "God's lioness,/ How one we grow." Significantly, the Greek work "Ariel," from the Hebrew word "Ariel," means "lioness of God." In the Bible it is a designation given by Isaiah to the city of Jerusalem, a city which is presently the object of God's wrath and condemned to tribulation, but which is promised deliverance in the apocalypse:

Woe to Ariel, to Ariel, the city where David dwelt! add ye year to year; let them kill sacrifices.

Yet I will distress Ariel, and there shall be heaviness and sorrow: and it shall be unto me as Ariel.

And I will camp against thee round about, and will lay seige against thee with a mount, and I will raise forts against thee. . . .

Moreover the multitude of thy strangers shall be like small dust, and the multitude of the terrible ones shall be as chaff that passeth away: yea, it shall be at an instant suddenly.

Thou shalt be visited of the Lord of hosts with thunder, and with earthquake, and great noise, with storm and tempest, and the flame of devouring fire.

And the multitude of all the nations that fight against Ariel, even all that fight against her and her munition, and that distress her, shall be as a dream of a night vision. (Isa. 29:1–3, 5–7)

Ariel, then, is poet, rider, and horse; she is a swift, indomitable presence galloping unflinchingly ahead; and she is an androgynous spirit assuming the form of anything, or anyone, who is oppressed and yearning for freedom. She is God's lioness. Ariel is also a specific poem and a volume of poetry, and in its unity of elements Ariel becomes also a metaphor for the poet's vision.

The poem's lines continue to display and define specific aspects of that vision:

> Nigger-eye
> Berries cast dark
> Hooks—
>
> Black sweet blood mouthfuls,
> Shadows.

The poet's present condition is indeed one of captivity and suffering; hooks, blackness, and darkness are familiar images which Plath uses elsewhere to express this. But inherent in the present misery is the expectation of its end. The suffering is merely prerequisite to release; the "black, blood mouthfuls" are "sweet."

This release has been anticipated from the poem's beginning, from the horse's first step into the "substanceless" landscape. All the while, forward motion has been intensifying; the powerful gallop is uncontrollable now, and Ariel seems to burst through the limits of earthly reality into a new, even more "substanceless" order:

> Something else
>
> Hauls me through air—
> Thighs, hair;
> Flakes from my heels.
>
> White
> Godiva, I unpeel—
> Dead hands, dead stringencies.
>
> And now I
> Foam to wheat, a glitter of seas.
> The child's cry
>
> Melts in the wall.

This is the purifying process of "Fever 103°" and "Tulips," the un-
peeling of "Lady Lazarus" and "Getting There." The "stringencies"
are "dead"; the hooks are at last powerless to detain her. The goal of
this ride is in sight; the "glitter" here, and the "dew" of the following
lines, is death, the dead bell's companion in "Death & Co.,"
the shimmering veil to be "let down" in "A Birthday Present,"
the "dewdrop" at the end of the journey in "Getting There." Even the
very kind of motion assumes death as the terminal. In "Years," the
poet confesses that

> What I love is
> The piston in motion—
> My soul dies before it.
> And the hooves of the horses,
> Their merciless churn.[8]

And we find the galloping hooves of "Ariel" in "Sheep in Fog" or
"Elm," the relentless motion of the piston in the Nazi train of "Get-
ting There" or in the train on which the secretary of "Three
Women," during her miscarriage, imagines herself:

> I am dying as I sit. I lose a dimension.
> Trains roar in my ears, departures, departures!
> The silver track of time empties into the distance,
> The white sky empties of its promise, like a cup.[9]

The poem's closing lines complete the flight and provide release.
Here, recognizable landscape is completely abandoned; surroundings seem more emotional than physical. As the move toward a pure
substanceless state is achieved, the fused identities of horse and
rider become an "arrow":

> And I
> Am the arrow,
>
> The dew that flies
> Suicidal, at one with the drive
> Into the red
>
> Eye, the cauldron of morning.

In these last lines one final element is aurally admitted into the unity which has been expanding through the poem. We see here that "I," which represents the oneness as it exists at this point, remains "at one with the drive." And merging with it is the "Eye," which is for one thing the bullseye, the target, the goal and end of this journey through present misery and tribulation. But it is also the veil which, penetrated, is the last barrier to apocalyptic triumph. It is both the redness of death and red morning sun, the light of a new day, of rebirth.

From its opening lines, then, the poem has proceeded inexorably toward this final breakthrough, so that the closing lines achieve both an ultimate shedding of tangibility and a complete unity of elements. There is also a rhythmic culmination in these lines. As we have previously noticed, the horse's gallop has been growing faster and more uncontrollable through the poem. And here, at the end, a kind of rhythmic climax is reached at exactly the moment that the last veil is rent. One way to trace this increase in intensity is by means of the poem's verbs; at first the earth only "splits and passes" the rider, but as speed increases she is "haul[ed] through air, she "Foam[s]," and finally she is "the arrow" that "flies/ Suicidal." The intensification of movement is traceable also in the poem's rhythms; the rhythms of "Ariel" are clearly sexual, much like the rhythms of "Fever 103°." Accordingly, the early cadences of the poem, where the speaker remains earthbound, are relatively calm; a shift occurs at the point where she breaks from earth and "Something else hauls me through air." From here on the lines grow shorter and the rhythms faster, increasing in tension toward the climactic "Eye." Release and resolution, "the cauldron of morning," follow immediately to end the poem.

This special release is characteristic not only of this poem but also of most of the other poems in *Ariel* and *Winter Trees* and indeed throughout Plath's canon. In one way or another, conveyed variously by certain images or by orgastic rhythms. Sylvia Plath expresses repeatedly the notions of present suffering and servitude, of violent and/or ecstatic death, and of triumph and new life as an immediate condition of that death. She is God's lioness; her vision is apocalyptic.

This is not to say, however, that she can forecast the exact nature of the new order or describe for us the particulars of the millennium. Of this her poetry gives only clues. What she does, instead, is descry present danger and woe, call attention to the tribulation of Jerusalem. She "warns," says Stephen Spender, which is "all a poet can do today." She manages to "turn our horrors and our achievements into the same witches' brew" until we are made to see that "a spaceman promenading in space is not too distant a relation from a man in a concentration camp, and that everything is a symptom of the same holocaust."[10] Yet in the very act of warning she anticipates the cataclysmic end of this present holocaust, and in so doing she becomes a herald of the apocalypse. David's city may presently be "visited . . . with thunder, and with earthquake, and great noise, with storm and tempest, and the flame of devouring fire," but it looks forward also to the time when "the multitude of all the nations that fight against Ariel, . . . and all that distress her, shall be as a dream of a night vision." (Isaiah 29:6.7)

In Plath's poems that night vision, the nightmare, assumes several identities. The tribulation of Ariel may appear as the anguish of Oedipus, the torture of the victimized Jew, the agony of ambivalent sexual attitudes, the grief of rejection, or the mother's poignant fear for her child. But whatever guise it assmes, the world of Ariel is the world of the nightmare in substance as well as in the surreal quality of its expression.

Apocalyptic release from the holocaust is both suicidal and ecstatic, and it always involves an act of purification, either religious, or fiery, or both. It is conveyed in several ways, one of which is by means of the phoenix symbol. In these late poems, the mention of ash, or the color red, or fire, or upward flight, dominate the closing lines, as, for example, in "Ariel": "Suicidal, at one with the drive/ Into the red/ Eye, the cauldron of morning" or "Lady Lazarus: "Out of the ash/ I rise with my red hair"[11] or "Stings":

> Now she is flying
> More terrible than she ever was, red
> Scar in the sky, red comet
> Over the engine that killed her—[12]

or "Fever 103°":

> I think I am going up,
> I think I may rise—
> The beads of hot metal fly, and I, love, I

> Am a pure acetylene
> Virgin
> Attended by roses,
> . . . .
>
> To Paradise.[13]

In its use of the Virgin, "Fever 103°" combines with the phoenix symbol another of the means Plath employs to express release or rebirth. The resurrected self may also be a totally pure, virginal woman. We see this also, for example, in "A Birthday Present":

> Is this the one for the annunciation?
> . . . .
>
> There would be nobility then, there would be a birthday.
> And the knife not carve, but enter
>
> Pure and clean as the cry of a baby,
> And the universe slide from my side.[14]

and in "Childless Woman": "This body,/ This ivory,/ Godly as a child's shriek."[15]

In their mention of the baby, "A Birthday Present" and "Childless Woman" show still another means Plath uses to convey the theme of release. As we saw in the transitional poem "Face-Lift," the poem's speaker may anticipate literal rebirth, may be "Mother to myself," in that case, the death day becomes also the birth day, and the birth is achieved in specific ways. In "A Birthday Present" the birth is Eve-like, "from my side." In "Getting There," the Speaker can "Step to you from the black car of Lethe,/ Pure as a baby." In "Mary's Song" it is the baby itself who faces death and sacramental resurrection ("O golden child the world will kill and eat"). The wife in "Three Women" expresses a similar attitude; about to give birth, she is "like a Mary." She is herself "sacrificial," but later fears for her baby boy, "swaddled in white bands." And in "Brasilia," the baby is "a nail/ Driven, driven in" by "you who eat/ People like light rays." In these poems, as in "Nick and the Candlestick," the baby, symbol of hope and new life for the mother, must himself suffer his present existence and anticipate apocalyptic release:

> The pain
> You wake to is not yours.
> . . . .
>
> You are the one
> Solid the spaces lean on, envious.
> You are the baby in the barn.[16]

Finally, the notion of death as a new beginning may be expressed in nuptial terms. In these poems, death day is not birth day but wedding day, as for example in "Little Fugue": "I survive the while,/ Arranging my morning. . . . / The clouds are a marriage dress, of that pallor;"[17] or "Winter Trees," with its "series of weddings," or in "Berck-Plage":

> A wedding-cake face in a paper frill.
> How superior he is now.
> . . . .
>
> And the bride flowers expend a freshness,
>
> And the soul is a bride
> In a still place, and the groom is red and forgetful,
> he is featureless.[18]

or in "Purdah," where the speaker who glitters like jade and "gleams like a mirror" awaits the bridegroom, "Lord of the mirrors," disturber of veils.

Such a metaphor is exactly appropriate in an apocalyptic vision such as Sylvia Plath's. In the Bible, marriage with the bridegroom Christ is an apocalyptic act for which all must prepare and wait, as expressed, for instance, in the parable of the ten virgins, where the five wise virgins, who remained watchful, "went in with him to the marriage": "Watch therefore, for ye know neither the day nor the hour wherein the Son of man cometh" (Matt. 25:1–13). Furthermore, in the Revelation of Saint John, this apocalyptic marriage includes Ariel specifically: "And I John saw the holy city, new Jerusalem, coming down from God out of heaven, prepared as a bride adorned for her husband" (Rev. 21:2). And it takes place to begin the millennium: "And the Spirit and the bride say, Come. And let him that heareth say, Come. And let him that is athirst

come. And whosoever will, let him take the water of life freely"
(Rev. 22:17).

Death is life, then, in Sylvia Plath's vision, and earthly life is
merely a prerequisite for death, often even a preparatory series of
small deaths. As Robert Scholes observes, Plath's "works do not
only come to us posthumously. They were written posthumously.
Between suicides."[19] As she anticipates variously her triumphal resurrection, her rebirth into a new and wholly pure form, and her
marriage, the poet is indeed Ariel, God's lioness.

CHAPTER 7

The Life in the Work

IN contemplating and judging such work, one may be keenly tempted to turn from an examination of the "posthumous" writing itself toward an analysis of the person who wrote it. Plath's poetry celebrates death, and we know that death is exactly and deliberately what the poet chose. Such knowledge, as in the case of any writer who has taken her or his own life, is difficult for us as readers to dismiss or ignore, for the fact of the writer's suicide informs and elucidates the words which we read as we read them. We undergo a similar experience and feel a similar curiosity, for instance, when we study the poems of Anne Sexton or John Berryman. If we are to see the work of any such writer clearly, however, we must realize that the author's death finally neither negates nor authenticates the work, for the poems do not die with the poet. Yet, if Sylvia Plath's art is not validated by her suicide, we may feel that the one appears to render the other more forthright, more genuine. She did what she said she would do.

Many readers want to know why she did it. Was her suicide a desperate cry for help, as some have suggested—even, perhaps, an act at which she intended to fail, as she had failed in her previous suicide attempt? Was it an ultimate act of denial from a person to whom life was onerous and impossible—perhaps, specifically, an act of female sacrifice in a male-dominated, victimizing world? Was Plath deranged, the tortured prey of some sort of manic-depressive syndrome which finally defeated her? Was her act a uniquely contemporary gesture, a horribly logical result of the kinds of imaginative risks which the vulnerable artists in our nihilistic modern society are forced to take?

Theories have been proposed. Those who see Plath's suicide as a uniquely contemporary gesture are also, generally those who see her as an important member of poetry's confessional movement.

108

Such a view does indeed offer an explanation of suicide in terms which we can discuss with some assurance, for it removes the act from the sort of personal, private realm where we are forced to deal with purely subjective or speculative materials, and places it in an accessible, objective context. If, in fact, Plath can accurately be considered a confessional poet, she is in the company of other famous poets also subject to periodic breakdown and sometimes eventual suicide—Hart Crane, Robert Lowell, John Berryman, Anne Sexton. Such similarity is not coincidental. Personal upheaval is not, however, a prerequisite for becoming a member of the confessional school; it is a threatened result. The confessional poet is one who, as the name implies, writes what appears to be personal confession, employing the self as the center of investigation and offering what seem to be supremely private revelations. But the confessional poet, in the specific and contemporary sense, is more than that; he or she is, as the poet M. L. Rosenthal has observed, one whose work is "highly charged" and who makes of the private psychological vulnerability at the poem's center a cultural symbol, an "embodiment of civilization."[1]

As well as the "confessional" label appears to suit Sylvia Plath's writing, however, there is some critical disagreement concerning her membership in that school. A number of observers, who believe that confessional writing is an isolated and solitary affair and that it therefore does not locate itself in a larger cultural context, claim that Plath is not a confessional poet. Confession, these critics argue, offers only pure expression of the anguish of the self or derangement, and Plath moves beyond anguish to prophecy and transmutes derangement into a myth for her age. Clearly, the disagreement here results from how one defines the term "confessional" in the first place. If, however, we assign the term "confessional" empirically, based upon our observation of the nature of the work of other unequivocally confessional writers (such as Crane, Lowell, Sexton, and Berryman), we shall include Plath in their numbers. For most critics agree upon the contemporary, cultural significance of all these poets' immediate, personal revelations.

Because of the very nature of this undertaking, then, as they dare to explore the dark and unknown realms of consciousness, such poets expose themselves to great emotional and psychological danger—as, for example, Plath does in her establishment of a metaphorical relationship between the quality of modern individual existence and such contemporary horrors as the atomic holocaust and the abomination of the concentration camp. Plath's suicide, says Rosenthal, "is part of the imaginative risk"[2] which contemporary artists must take.

Another theory to explain Sylvia Plath's sense of victimization and her suicide is offered in an essentially feminist context. Certainly there is in Sylvia Plath's work an expression of rage against men which escalates, sometimes, to a hatred of their oppressive power, a quality which has led a number of feminists to claim Plath as a major spokeswoman for their cause. Plath's expressed attitudes in any volume of her poetry do indeed lend credence to this view; as we have seen in *Ariel*, for instance, the woman is man's prey, tormented beyond endurance by what she perceives as his impossible demands or reduced to the role of lifeless puppet by his destructive expectations. Even a partial survey of the *Ariel* poems underscores the point. In "The Applicant," the woman being offered as a wife is totally dehumanized, a "living doll," an "it" reduced to pure function: "It can sew, it can cook,/ It can talk, talk, talk." In "The Rival," where the poem's very title defines the female–male relationship, the man is "beautiful, but annihilating." The speaker of "Lady Lazarus" is, in one of her guises, similar to the "living doll" of "The Applicant"; she is a circus freak lady performing her act, "the big strip tease." Under the napkin she is really a corpse which can "terrify" her audience by revealing "the nose, the eye pits, the full set of teeth," but she is nevertheless forced to conclude her act by playing the "smiling woman." In this poem, all male figures are the adversary; whether they are "Herr Doktor," the Nazi victimizer, or "Herr God," or "Herr Lucifer," they are all one "Herr Enemy." But in this poem also the woman-victim warns of her revenge: "Beware . . . I eat men like air." The terrible Nazi figure appears often in Plath's poetry; the Jew is his prey, and the woman thus assumes that role. In "Daddy," this "man in black with a Meinkampf look" is husband as well as father, a "bastard" whom the woman has had to kill. But the woman has not found release in her oppressor's death; inextricably bound to her captor, she has been forced to "[try] to die" to "get back" to him.

To be sure, the materials and the texture of male oppression are vividly rendered in Sylvia Plath's work, in her prose as well as her poetry. Esther Greenwood of *The Bell Jar* may be seen, to a point, as the quintessential victim of a male-dominated society. Her confusion and breakdown result from her inability to integrate the conventional wisdom which has been externally imposed upon her with her most basic personal instincts. Those people like Mrs. Willard and her mother who have thoroughly conditioned her sexual expectations are the most unliberated of women; Esther's role options, as she has learned them from women like these, are singularly unappealing to her. Esther can see no satisfactory self-fulfillment in female subservience and domestic submission; yet, because she has lacked a liberated role model and is too insecure to forge one for herself, she is cornered into increasing immobility. The female Dr. Nolan finally offers Esther the example and the help she needs to build a new, liberated personality, as well as the strength to deal with the guilt which accompanies her discarding of the mother–Mrs. Willard norms. Esther's eventual marriage represents, perhaps, the measure of her successful liberation; we are encouraged to assume that matrimony and motherhood, once her nemesis, no longer hinder her emancipated self-fulfillment. Yet this conclusion is not certain; it may be that Esther's eventual marriage represents not success, but failure to liberate herself. Indeed, many feminists see marriage as a cop-out; and for Esther, it may herald the redescent of her stifling bell jar.

To be sure, if Sylvia Plath does express a feminist point of view in her writing, it does not seem to be of the variety which offers a viable program for release from and overcoming of male oppression. She may offer an affecting portrait of the destruction and loss which that oppression creates, and in so doing may explore matters coincidental with feminist concerns. But Plath does not finally, as a writer or as a person, seem predominantly interested in advancing the feminist cause. Her hatred of men seems rooted not so much in feminism as in her deeply disabling, ambivalent relationship with her father; it seems frivolous to say that her struggle with the colossus expresses merely a feminist's sense of sexual injustice.

Indeed, the attitude toward men which emerges from her writing is a love-hate relationship; the destruction of her male oppressors requires also the destruction of herself. The only way for the speaker of her poems to deny the male victimizer, the only way not to be a victim, is to reject or destroy him altogether. But in so doing—in refusing, for example, to be the Applicant's "living doll"—she places herself in an equally impossible position, victimizing herself. For she is now condemned to an equally hateful existence of solitariness, chastity, and loneliness. As she says in "Elm," love may be terrifying and murderous; it kills; but she is also, as she recoils, "Inhabited by a cry" which looks "for something to love." In "Fever 103°" the "low smokes" of love and passion "roll" from her "like Isadora's scarves," and, like those scarves, they may kill her. "O love, O celibate," exclaims the speaker of "Letter in November"; she walks through a golden landscape where all the golds are "mouths of Thermopylae," gates so well defended that the enemy love has no chance to enter. Death and love go together. The need for love inevitably leads to figurative or actual death. Or, like Elizabeth Minton and the speaker of "Daddy," the woman must join her murdered lover-oppressor in death.

There is, actually, evidence that Plath had little personal interest in the feminist cause. In her own marriage, she chose for herself a role of domestic submissiveness, while placing the success of her husband's career above her own. She seems to have performed her various duties as housewife conscientiously and well; she was a devoted mother, a good cook, and a thorough housekeeper. It may perhaps be true that a significant motivating factor in Plath's conjugal submission and domestic energy was her perfectionist tendency, the habit established early in her life of devoting her full energies to the performing of any task set before her. And, in that regard, it is even likely that Plath's freedom to set priorities for her own marriage was limited by her earlier background and conditioning, specifically by the example and influence of her mother.

Nevertheless, however her priorities may have been predetermined, Sylvia Plath acted in ways consistent with her present character. She did rebel from time to time; we know, for example, that Plath occasionally resented the restrictions which her chosen wifely role imposed upon her. She regretted the fact that infant care with its attendant domestic duties left her little time to write, and she was bothered that she had no close personal friend. Perhaps the most significant measure of Plath's dissatisfaction with her conjugal situation was one of her responses to its collapse. After her separation from her husband, even though she had to continue keeping house and caring for her children, she began to write poems daily, urgently—as she said, as if domesticity had choked her. One has the feeling that Plath was, at this time, at the edge of conscious feminist awareness—that she might, had she lived longer, have been able to build from the wreckage of her marriage a self-reliant, clearly feminist point of view. But this is merely conjecture; she did not. And in life she appears to have shown no actively feminist predilections.

It may be that we can derive at least a partial understanding of Sylvia Plath's despair and self-destructiveness simply by studying what she wrote. We have seen already, and in some detail, the nature of Plath's sense of oppression and thralldom, the components of her debilitating inner conflicts, and her felt necessity for release and/or revenge. For Sylvia Plath as for Esther Greenwood, purity remained the great issue. We know from reading Plath's poetry and fiction and letters that she was tormented by the strumpet-spinster conflict, and we infer from her searing examination of this conflict that she was tormented as well by her very keen awareness of it, by her unrelenting consciousness. As she wrote in "Elm," "I am incapable of more knowledge." We know that Plath's perfectionism continually assured for her a sense of failure. And we can discover from close personal observers like Nancy Hunter Steiner that Plath's first suicide attempt was born partly from that very sense of failure and partly from a desperate need to bring an end to her tortured consciousness, from a depression that "resulted from an inability to maintain a sense of her own worth, particularly in the face of the high praise others invariably heaped upon her."[3] We might go on to apply these gathered bits of information to Plath's second, successful suicide attempt, and surmise the reasons for her need to "efface" herself, as she put it in the late poem "Tulips." But what we would have then would be at best a theory, not an unequivocal explanation.

For art is not life. As Sylvia Plath herself wrote, though her poems are derived from her "sensuous and emotional experiences," they are changed and transformed in the poem, manipulated and controlled, objectified and made relevant. Everywhere in Plath's work we can find evidence of this informing, formalizing process at work, evidence which reveals the sorts of distortions of life that such a process must necessarily entail. For example, in *The Bell Jar*, it is the newly deflowered Esther Greenwood who presents Irwin with the hospital bill for medical services resulting from their sexual encounter. For the reader, this is an event which underscores Esther's emotional recovery; we cheer her newfound strength and courage. If she can do that, we say to ourselves, she surely will have the perspective and sense to endure future difficulty, to stand her ground. Plath no doubt has written this scene in this way to invite precisely such a response. But Sylvia Plath is not Esther Greenwood. We learn from Nancy Hunter Steiner, Plath's roommate and companion through this ordeal, that though such an event did take place, the strong and sensible woman was Steiner herself. Plath, in reality, felt extremely frightened and insecure; Steiner took her to the hospital and directed the bill to Irwin.

This Esther-Sylvia-Irwin incident may be minor, but it proves the point. We err if we fail to observe the necessary distinctions between art and life. Such observance is more easily accomplished when we can see the distinction, as in the hospital bill episode. But even when we lack the information to make such a comparison, we must allow the principle. Other examples seem perhaps more central to our understanding of Plath's consciousness. Mrs. Greenwood in *The Bell Jar* is represented as an insensitive, selfish, demanding, smothering woman. Aurelia Plath no doubt served as her model; we can infer from reading Sylvia Plath's letters together with Aurelia Plath's editorial comments that the real-life mother was, at least, ambitious for her daughter and, perhaps, somewhat cold. But between the two mothers there is interposed the glass of fictional distortion. At the time she wrote *The Bell Jar,* Plath may indeed have felt this way about her mother, and that insight, in itself, is valuable. Yet the one mother is not the other. Biography can be known only dimly through the artist's perception of it.

The father offers another example. Patricide is readily apparent in many of Plath's poems; again and again, the daughter-speaker claims either that she was responsible for her father's death or that she actually murdered him; as she says in "Daddy," "I have had to kill you." In other poems she assumes the guise of Oedipus, or Orestes, or Electra, or simply an orphan. Actually, as we know, Plath's father died of natural causes, after an illness of several years' duration. Once again, what is important here is the insight afforded by the poet's manipulation of life. Nancy Hunter Steiner reveals Plath's motive. Plath confessed, says Steiner, that " 'He was an autocrat. . . . I adored and despised him, and I probably wished many times that he were dead. When he obliged me and died, I imagined that I had killed him.' "[4]

What, then, was the source of Sylvia Plath's final undoing? Why did she die? The question is one which no one can answer conclusively; even if we had been there, we likely would have no final answer. Plath may indeed have intended for her suicide attempt to fail, but it did not. A life which she chose to end must truly have been onerous and impossible for her, but we can only speculate upon her reasons for such an ultimate denial. A confessional poet she should no doubt be considered; a full-fledged feminist she should not. But locating her in one school or another serves primarily a literary critical rather than a biographical purpose; it is difficult to see an abstract, cultural "imaginative risk" as sufficient motivation for real suicide. She may have suffered some recurrent, debilitating mental illness, but that is a diagnosis which we are neither equipped nor at liberty to make.

For Sylvia Plath the poet, the materials of biography are meaningful principally for the artistic uses she makes of them, and her perceptions become important to us, her readers, not because they re-create the person, but because they create the art. What is available for our certain scrutiny is not the person but the poetry; Plath's death neither negates nor authenticates her work in the sense that her poems of apocalyptic vision survive her, speaking powerfully and compellingly to whoever may read them. Her late poems assure her a place among poets; she is a fine writer no matter how or at what age she died. Therefore, the most rewarding perspective which we, as readers and witnesses, can assume is one whose main focus is the self newly created for us, phoenixlike, in the poetry. With this viewpoint, we realize that the woman in the poems is the Sylvia Plath who is Ariel, God's lioness.

With the poems as evidence, we may explore and analyze as much as we please. Sylvia Plath's interest in death may indeed be personal and private, but it is also the paramount thematic concern in her poetry. Her preoccupation with death is not only isolated and solitary; it is imaginative and metaphorical. And an examination of Plath's attitudes toward death, in her poems, reveals the nature of her vision: it is apocalyptic.

To see Plath as Ariel is to provide both motivation and the tools for examination. Ariel in her mundane existence is troubled; she lives the only life which is possible for her but which casts her in the impossible role of servant and victim. Like Jerusalem, she is beseiged; the storm and tempest and devouring fire which distress that city afflict her as well. She is a Jew, victim of grim atrocities. She is a woman, victim of a sexual passion which can realize neither viable release nor proper partner. She is a mother, servant to a solitary and fearful parenthood.

Like Jerusalem as well, her expectations are supramundane. Death signals the end of her distress and promises a new existence in which the enemies of Ariel will be punished. But it is also a cataclysmic occurrence whose outcome denies earthly certification. Therefore death is a goal at once intensely desired and greatly feared. At the same time ecstatic and agonized, Ariel gallops, flies, or speeds unflinchingly toward it.

Death is an annealing, transfiguring experience. From it the woman may rise, shedding "dead hands, dead stringencies," to an ecstatic, totally pure union with the Spirit. Sexual ambivalence is resolved in the choice of this marriage partner; he is both Christ the son and God the father, apocalyptic analogues of the choices she has made, but cannot decide between, in earthly life. In death, too, the baby is assured the same eventual triumph. And from death the phoenix may rise to live again.

Essentially Christian in its outlines, this apocalyptic vision belongs wholly to the poet. Sylvia Plath's poetry is not religious in any strict, literal sense; it is not a vehicle to redisclose the vision of Isaiah and Saint John. Plath's use of biblical materials, like her use of mythical and biographical ones, is metaphorical, a means by which she creates and expresses her individual, compelling vision. Like the poems themselves, the self who emerges from these poems has the energy, strength, and womanly instincts of a lioness, and the death-defying perspective of one who is God's. The poems are not prophetic but apocalyptic; as Sylvia Plath herself tells us, "I am not gifted with the tongue of Jeremiah, though I may be sleepless enough before my vision of the apocalypse."[5]

Notes and References

Chapter One

1. Sylvia Plath, *Letters Home*, ed. Aurelia Schober Plath (New York, 1975), p. 346; hereafter cited in text as *L*.
2. Nancy Hunter Steiner, *A Closer Look at Ariel: A Memory of Sylvia Plath* (New York, 1973), p. 57.
3. *The Bell Jar* (New York, 1971), p. 275; hereafter cited in text as *B*.
4. *The Savage God* (New York, 1971), p. 6.

Chapter Two

1. *The Bell Jar*, p. 23.

Chapter Three

1. Hughes, "The Chronological Order of Sylvia Plath's Poems," in *The Art of Sylvia Plath*, ed. Charles Newman (Bloomington, 1970), p. 187.
2. "Temper of Time," *The Nation*, 181 (August 6, 1955), 119.
3. "Departure," in *The Colossus* (New York, 1962), p. 18.
4. "Lament," *New Orleans Poetry Journal*, 1 (October, 1955), 19.
5. "Wreath for a Bridal," *Poetry*, 89 (January, 1957), 231.
6. "The Other Two," in *Lyonnesse* (London, 1971), p. 26.
7. "Crystal Gazer," in *Crystal Gazer* (London, 1917), pp. 17–18.
8. "Admonitions," *Smith Review*, Spring, 1954, p. 23.
9. "Metamorphoses of the Moon," in *Lyonnesse*, pp. 8–9.
10. "Black Rook in Rainy Weather," in *Crossing the Water* (New York, 1971), p. 41.
11. "Sylvia Plath and Confessional Poetry," in *The Art of Sylvia Plath*, p. 71.
12. "To Eva Descending the Stair," *Harper's Magazine*, 209 (September, 1954), 63.
13. "Doomsday," *Harper's Magazine*, 208 (May, 1954), 29.
14. "The Dream of the Hearse-Driver," in *Crystal Gazer*, p. 10.
15. "Ocean 1212–W," *The Listener* 70 (August 29, 1963), 313.
16. Sylvia Plath, "Circus in Three Rings," *Atlantic Monthly*, 196 (August, 1955), p. 68.

17. "A Winter's Tale," *New Yorker*, 35 (December 12, 1959), 116.

18. " 'Some god got hold of me,' " *Village Voice*, 16 (October 28, 1971), 30.

19. "Metaphors," in *Crossing the Water*, p. 43.

20. "Tinker Jack and the Tidy Wives," *Accent*, 17 (Autumn, 1957), 248.

21. "Ocean 1212-W," p. 313.

22. "Electra on Azalea Path," *Hudson Review*, 13 (Fall, 1960), 414–15.

23. "Sunday at the Mintons'," *Mademoiselle*, 35 (August, 1952), 377.

24. Ibid., 255.

25. "Maenad," *Crossing the Water*, p. 51.

26. "Candor Is the Only Wile—The Art of Sylvia Plath," in *The Art of Sylvia Plath*, p. 23.

27. Hughes, "The Chronological Order," p. 192.

Chapter Four

1. "The Poetry of Sylvia Plath—A Technical Analysis," in *The Art of Sylvia Plath*, pp. 140–52.

2. Ibid., pp. 147–48, 151–52.

3. "On Three Women," in *The Art of Sylvia Plath*, pp. 227–29.

4. *The Art of Sylvia Plath*, p. 60.

5. *The Poet Speaks*, ed. Peter Orr (London, 1966), p. 170.

6. "Mayflower," in *Lyonnesse*, p. 3.

7. *Wreath for a Bridal* (Frensham, 1970), unpaged.

8. *Crystal Gazer*, p. 14.

9. Nims, p. 140.

10. Snakecharmer, "The Hermit at Outermost House," in *The Colossus*, pp. 9, 54.

11. *Crossing the Water* (New York, 1971), pp. 10–11.

12. *Winter Trees*, (New York, 1972), p. 16.

13. "The Genie in the Bottle," in *Mid Century American Poets*, ed. John Ciardi (New York, 1950), p. 7.

14. *New York Times Book Review*, October 10, 1971, pp. 4, 48.

15. *Winter Trees*, pp. 37–39.

16. Ibid., p. 19.

17. Ibid., pp. 4–5.

18. "Warnings from the Grave," *New Republic*, 154 (June 18, 1966), p. 23.

19. "Kindness," in *Ariel* (New York, 1966), p. 82.

Chapter Five

1. Hughes, "The Chronological Order," p. 192.

2. Ted Hughes, "Note," in *Winter Trees*.

3. Ibid.

4. "Warnings from the Grave," p. 23.

5. *The Poet Speaks*, pp. 169–70.

6. Ibid., p. 169.

7. "Warning from the Grave," p. 25.

8. *Ariel* (New York, 1966), pp. 36–38.

9. "Necessity and Freedom: The Poetry of Robert Lowell, Sylvia Plath, and Anne Sexton," *Critical Quarterly*, 7 (Spring, 1965), 22.

10. *Winter Trees* (New York, 1972), pp. 2–7

11. "Ocean 1212–W," p. 312.

12. *The Art of Sylvia Plath*, p. 66.

13. "On 'Daddy,' " in *The Art of Sylvia Plath*, pp. 235–36.

14. "Warnings from the Grave," p. 25.

15. *The Art of Sylvia Plath*, p. 229.

16. "Context," *London Magazine*, February, 1962, p. 46.

17. "Foreword," in *Ariel*, p. ix.

18. "The Barfly Ought to Sing," in *The Art of Sylvia Plath*, p. 175.

19. "Context," p. 46.

Chapter Six

1. "Ariel," in *Ariel*, p. 26.

2. *The Art of Sylvia Plath*, p. 61.

3. Hughes, p. 194.

4. William Shakespeare, *The Tempest*, act 1, sc. 2, lines 242–46, 495–97.

5. "The Hanging Man," in *Ariel*, p. 69.

6. "Three Women: A Poem for Three Voices," in *Winter Trees*, p. 50.

7. "Purdah," in *Winter Trees*, p. 42.

8. "Years," in *Ariel*, p. 72.

9. "Three Women: A Poem for Three Voices," in *Winter Trees*, p. 48.

10. "Warnings from the Grave," p. 26.

11. "Lady Lazarus," in *Ariel*, p. 9.

12. "Stings," in *Ariel*, p. 63.

13. "Fever 103°," in *Ariel*, pp. 54–5.

14. "A Birthday Present," in *Ariel*, pp. 42, 44.

15. "Childless Woman," in *Winter Trees*, p. 34.

16. "Nick and the Candlestick," in *Ariel*, p. 34.

17. "Little Fugue," in *Ariel*, p. 71.

18. "Berck-Plage," in *Ariel*, pp. 22, 25.

19. Robert Scholes, "The Bell Jar," *New York Times Book Review*, April 11, 1971, p. 7.

Chapter Seven

1. *The Art of Sylvia Plath*, p. 69.

2. Ibid., p. 74.

3. Nancy Hunter Steiner, p. 63.
4. Ibid., pp. 62–63.
5. "Context," p. 46.

Selected Bibliography

PRIMARY SOURCES

This listing, arranged by genre (section I, poetry; section II, fiction; section III, nonfiction), includes both books by Sylvia Plath published as separate volumes and shorter published works (poems, stories, essays and interviews) which are to date uncollected. Because the contents of the British and American editions of all four of Plath's commercially published poetry volumes differ, publication information is given for each edition. In addition to the poems collected in these commercial volumes and in the limited-edition volumes, there are thirteen poems which appear in the Appendix to Charles Newman's *The Art of Sylvia Plath;* four of these appear in no other collection, and one, "Miss Drake Proceeds to Supper," is published nowhere else. There remain, finally, thirty-three uncollected poems; these are listed separately. Plath's published short stories, as well as her published nonfiction, so far uncollected, are listed individually as well.

I Poetry

A. Books

Ariel. London: Faber and Faber Ltd., 1965; New York: Harper & Row, Publishers, Inc., 1966.

The Colossus and Other Poems. London: William Heinemann Ltd., 1960; New York: Alfred A. Knopf, 1962; London: Faber and Faber Ltd., 1976.

Crossing the Water. London: Faber and Faber Ltd., 1971; New York: Harper & Row, Publishers, Inc., 1971.

Crystal Gazer. London: Rainbow Press, 1971. Limited edition of 400 copies.

Lyonnesse. London: Rainbow Press, 1971. Limited edition of 400 copies.

Three Women, A Monologue for Three Voices. London: Turret Books, 1968. Limited edition of 180 copies. Subsequently included in *Winter Trees.*

Uncollected Poems. London: Turret Books, 1965. Limited edition of 150 copies.

121

Winter Trees. London: Faber and Faber Ltd., 1971; New York: Harper & Row, Publishers, Inc., 1972.
Wreath for a Bridal. Frensham: The Sceptre Press, 1970. Limited edition of 100 copies.

B. Uncollected Poems

"Admonition," *Smith Review,* Spring, 1954, p. 3. *Harvard Advocate,* 101 (May, 1967), 2–3.
"Aerialist," *Cambridge Review,* 90 (February 7, 1969), 245.
"Apotheosis," *The Lyric,* Winter, 1956, p. 10.
"Bitter Strawberries," *Christian Science Monitor,* August, 1950.
"Complaint of the Crazed Queen," *Times Literary Supplement,* 68 (July 31, 1969), 855.
"Danse Macabre," *Smith Review,* Spring, 1955, p. 12. *Harvard Advocate,* 101 (May, 1967), 2–3.
"The Death of Myth-Making," *Poetry,* 94 (September, 1959), 370. *Tri-Quarterly,* 7 (Fall, 1966), 11.
"Denouement," *Smith Review,* Spring, 1954, p. 23.
"Doomsday," *Smith Review,* Spring, 1953, p. 22. *Harper's Magazine,* 208 (May, 1954), 29.
"Dream with Clam Diggers," *Poetry,* 89 (January, 1957), 232–33. *Granta,* 61 (March 9, 1957), 5.
"Ella Mason and Her Eleven Cats," *Poetry,* 90 (July, 1957), 233–34.
"The Fearful," *The Observer,* February 17, 1963, p. 23.
"Fiesta Melons," *Christian Science Monitor,* July 31, 1959, p. 8.
"The Jailer," *Encounter,* 21 (October, 1963), 47–48.
"A Lesson in Vengeance," *Poetry,* 94 (September, 1959), 371.
"Letter to a Purist," *Times Literary Supplement,* 68 (July 31, 1969), 855.
"Main Street at Midnight," *The Spectator,* 102 (February 13, 1959), 227.
"Natural History," *Cambridge Review,* 90 (February 7, 1969), 244–45.
"The Net Menders," *New Yorker,* 36 (August 20, 1960), 36.
"November Graveyard," *Mademoiselle,* 62 (November, 1965), 134.
"On the Decline of Oracles," *Poetry,* 94 (September, 1959), 368–69.
"Prologue to Spring," *Christian Science Monitor,* March 26, 1959, p. 8.
"Pursuit," *Atlantic Monthly,* 199 (January, 1957), 65.
"Resolve," *Granta,* 61 (March 9, 1957), 5. *Cambridge Review,* 90 (February 7, 1969), 244–45.
"Second Winter," *The Lyric,* Winter, 1956, p. 11. *Ladies' Home Journal,* 75 (December, 1958), 143.
"The Sleepers," *London Magazine,* 7 (June, 1960), 11.
"Soliloquy of the Solipsist," *Granta,* 61 (May 4, 1957), 19.
"Song for Summer Day," *Christian Science Monitor,* August 18, 1959, p. 8.
"Southern Sunrise," *Christian Science Monitor,* August 26, 1959, p. 8.
"Street Song," *Cambridge Review,* 90 (February 7, 1969), 244.

"Temper of Time," *The Nation,* 181 (August 6, 1955), 119.
"To Eva Descending the Stair," *Harper's Magazine,* 209 (September, 1954), 63.
"Two Lovers and a Beachcomber by the Real Sea," *Mademoiselle,* 41 (August, 1955), 52, 62. *Granta,* 61 (March 9, 1957), 5.

II *Fiction*

A. Book

The Bell Jar. London: William Heinemann Ltd., 1963 (published under pseudonym Victoria Lucas); London: Faber and Faber Ltd., 1966; New York: Harper & Row, Publishers, Inc., 1971; and New York: Bantam Books, 1972 (with author identified).

B. Short Stories

"And Summer Will Not Come Again," *Seventeen,* March, 1950.
"The Daughters of Blossom Street," *London Magazine,* 7 (May, 1960), 34–48.
"The Day Mr. Prescott Died," *Granta,* 60 (October 20, 1956), 20–23.
"The Fifteen-Dollar Eagle," *Sewanee Review,* 68 (Autumn, 1960), 603–18.
"The Fifty-Ninth Bear," *London Magazine,* 8 (February, 1961), 11–20.
"In the Mountains," *Smith Review,* Fall, 1954, 2–5.
"Johnny Panic and the Bible of Dreams," *Atlantic Monthly,* 222 (September, 1968), 54–60.
"The Mothers' Union," *McCall's,* 100 (October, 1972), 80–81, 126–30, 142.
"Sunday At the Mintons' " *Mademoiselle,* 35 (August, 1952), 255, 371–78. *Smith Review,* Fall, 1962, 3–9.
"Superman and Paula Brown's New Snowsuit," *Smith Review,* Spring, 1955, 19–21.
"What I Found Out About Buddy Willard," *McCall's,* 98 (April, 1971), 86–87. (Excerpt from *The Bell Jar.*)
"The Wishing Box," *Granta,* 61 (January 26, 1957), 3–5, *Atlantic Monthly,* 214 (October 1964), 86–89.

III *Nonfiction*

A. Book

Letters Home, ed. Aurelia Schober Plath. New York: Harper & Row, Publishers, Inc., 1975.

B. Articles, Essays, Interviews

"Context," *London Magazine,* n.s. 1 (February, 1962), 45–6.
"Eccentricity," *The Listener,* 79 (May 9, 1968), 607.
"Mademoiselle's Last Word on College," *Mademoiselle,* 37 (August, 1953), 235.
"Oblongs," *New Statesman,* 63 (May 18, 1962), 724 [review].

"Ocean 1212–W," *The Listener*, 70 (August 29, 1963), 312–13. *Writers on Themselves*, ed. Herbert Read, London: Cox and Wyman Ltd., 1964. *The Art of Sylvia Plath*, ed. Charles Newman. Bloomington: Indiana University Press, 1970.

"The Poet Speaks," BBC interview, Argo records. Also published in *The Poet Speaks*, ed. Peter Orr. London: Routledge & Kegan Paul Ltd., 1966.

"Pair of Queens," *New Statesman*, 63 (April 27, 1962), 602–603. [review].

"Poets on Campus," *Mademoiselle*, 37 (August, 1953), 235.

"Sketchbook of a Spanish Summer," *Christian Science Monitor*, November 5, 1956, p. 13, and November 6, 1956, p. 17.

SECONDARY SOURCES

I *Bibliography*

HOMBERGER, ERIC. A *Chronological Checklist of the Periodical Publications of Sylvia Plath*. Exeter, England: F. E. Raddan and Sons Limited, 1970. American Arts Pamphlet Series, published by the American Arts Documentation Centre at the University of Exeter. This is a checklist of all poems, short stories, and nonfiction by Sylvia Plath published in periodicals between 1950 and 1969.

KINZIE, MARY. "An Informal Check List of Criticism," *The Art of Sylvia Plath*, ed. Charles Newman. Bloomington and London: Indiana University Press, 1970. An annotated list of Plath criticism published between 1960 and 1967.

NORTHOUSE, CAMERON, and WALSH, THOMAS P. *Sylvia Plath and Anne Sexton: A Reference Guide*. Boston: G. K. Hall & Co., 1974. A listing of poetry and prose (fiction and nonfiction) by Sylvia Plath published in periodical and in book form between 1952 and 1973, followed by a selected, annotated listing of books and articles about Sylvia Plath published between 1960 and 1973.

II *Criticism and Biography*

A. Books

AIRD, EILEEN. *Sylvia Plath: Her Life and Work*. New York: Harper & Row, Publishers, Inc., 1973. A general study of Plath's writing. For easy reference, separate chapters provide a short biography (Chap. 1), studies of each of Plath's commercially published volumes of poetry (Chaps. 2–5), an analysis of *The Bell Jar* (Chap. 6), and a general examination of the "interrelated symbols and image clusters" which Plath uses most frequently (Chap. 7).

ALVAREZ, A. *The Savage God.* New York: Random House, 1971. A study of suicide and the artist's special vulnerability to it. Part One focuses on Sylvia Plath specifically; the rest of the book mentions her here and there.

BUTSCHER, EDWARD. *Sylvia Plath: Method and Madness.* New York: Seabury Press, Inc., 1975. This critical biography offers a significant contribution to Plath scholarship. Clearly, much thorough research informs this detailed account of Plath's life (a few photographs are included). Butscher's aim, in which he succeeds admirably, is to show "the dynamic interaction between self and art at work."

HOLBROOK, DAVID. *Sylvia Plath: Poetry and Existence.* Atlantic Highlands, New Jersey: Humanities Press, Inc., 1976. This most interesting book offers a psychological study of Plath both as an individual and as a contemporary artist as a means of providing insight into her poetry.

KROLL, JUDITH. *Chapters in a Mythology: The Poetry of Sylvia Plath.* New York: Harper & Row, Publishers, Inc., 1976. A study of the "thematic meaning of Plath's late poems." This book is especially useful for its discussion of Plath's imagery, for its exploration of her mythic and literary sources, and for its close reading of several specific poems.

MELANDER, INGRID. *The Poetry of Sylvia Plath: A Study of Themes.* Stockholm: Almquist & Wiksell, 1972. Gothenburg Studies in English 25. This book offers a thematic analysis of Plath's poetry. Three basic themes are examined: the relationship between father and daughter, the sense of estrangement from or hostility in nature, and death.

NEWMAN, CHARLES, ed. *The Art of Sylvia Plath.* Bloomington and London: Indiana University Press, 1970. A most useful collection of articles about Sylvia Plath, including critical essays about Plath's poetry and novel, biographical essays, and reviews. The appendix includes a selection of Plath's work, some of Plath's pen drawings, and a bibliography. Many excellent critical essays on Plath, which appeared originally in journals, are reprinted in this book; these are not listed in IIB (Criticism and Biography: Essays and Reviews). Contents: Charles Newman, "Candor Is the Only Wile—The Art of Sylvia Plath" (pp. 21–55); A. Alvarez, "Sylvia Plath" (pp. 56–68); M. L. Rosenthal, "Sylvia Plath and Confessional Poetry" (pp. 69–76); Richard Howard, "Sylvia Plath: 'And I have No Face, I Have Wanted to Efface Myself . . . ' " pp. 77–88); Edward Lucie-Smith, "Sea-imagery in the Work of Sylvia Plath" (pp. 91–99); Annette Lavers, "The World as Icon—On Sylvia Plath's Themes" (pp. 100–35); John Frederick Nims, "The Poetry of Sylvia Plath—A Technical Analysis" (pp. 136–52); Lois Ames, "Notes toward a Biography" (pp. 155–73); Anne Sexton, "The Barfly Ought to Sing" (pp. 174–81); Wendy Campbell, "Remembering Sylvia" (pp. 182–86); Ted Hughes, "The Chronological Order of Sylvia Plath's

Poems" (pp. 187–95); Stephen Spender, "Warnings from the Grave" (pp. 199–203); A. E. Dyson, "On Sylvia Plath" (pp. 204–10); George Steiner, "Dying Is an Art" (pp. 211–18); Mary Ellmann, "The Bell Jar—An American Girlhood" (pp. 221–26); Douglas Cleverdon, "On Three Women" (pp. 227–29); A. R. Jones, "On 'Daddy' " (pp. 230–36); Appendix.

STEINER, NANCY HUNTER. A Closer Look at Ariel: A Memory of Sylvia Plath. New York: Popular Library, 1973. An insightful and valuable memoir of Plath's college years by her college roommate, with an excellent introduction by George Stade.

B. Essays and Reviews

CLAIRE, WILLIAM F. "That Rare, Random Descent: The Poetry and Pathos of Sylvia Plath," Antioch Review, 26 (Winter, 1966), 552–60. An exploration of Plath's uniquely modern and confessional qualities.

COOLEY, PETER. "Autism, Autoeroticism, Auto-da-fe: The Tragic Poetry of Sylvia Plath," Hollins Critic, 10 (February, 1973), 1–15. A review by an important contemporary poet of Plath's early, transitional, and late poems, with special attention given to the persona in Ariel.

COX, C. B., and JONES, A. R. "After the Tranquillized Fifties: Notes on Sylvia Plath and James Baldwin," Critical Quarterly, 6 (Summer, 1964), 107–22. This is an important essay in Plath criticism, for it marks a very early, wholly serious approach to her as an artist. A portion was later reprinted as "On Daddy" by Jones in The Art of Sylvia Plath.

DAVISON, PETER. 'Inhabited by a Cry': The Last Poetry of Sylvia Plath," Atlantic Monthly, 218 (August, 1966), 76–77. A brief but useful Ariel review. With these late poems as evidence, Davison praises the maturity of Plath's art, noting that her work's highly emotional quality should not obscure the fact that "a true poet" wrote it. Her poems "are a triumph for poetry, in fact, at the moment that they are a defeat for their author."

HARDWICK, ELIZABETH. "On Sylvia Plath," New York Review of Books, 17 (August 12, 1971), 3–6. Reviewing The Bell Jar and Crossing the Water, Hardwick examines Plath's predominant attitudes and themes, paying special attention to her fascination with death.

HIMELICK, RAYMOND. "Notes on the Care and Feeding of Nightmares: Burton, Erasmus, and Sylvia Plath," Western Humanities Review, 28 (Autumn, 1974), 313–26. A study of the ways in which The Bell Jar, while generically similar to Burton's Anatomy of Melancholy and Erasmus's In Praise of Folly, projects a uniquely twentieth-century sensibility.

HOLBROOK, DAVID. "R. D. Laing and the Death Circuit," Encounter, 31 (August, 1968), 34–45. A psychoanalytic approach concerned with theories of sanity and suicide. This essay examines Plath's emphasis on death as a means of rebirth.

HOWE, IRVING. "Sylvia Plath: A Partial Disagreement," *Harper's Magazine* (January, 1972), 88–91. A provocative essay which suggests that Plath's work does not merit the critical acclaim it had recently received.

JONES, A. R. "Necessity and Freedom: The Poetry of Robert Lowell, Sylvia Plath, and Anne Sexton," *Critical Quarterly*, 7 (Spring 1965), 11–30. Of major significance in this essay is Jones's use and definition of the term "confessional" and his early consideration of a "confessional" movement in modern American poetry.

LIBBY, ANTHONY. "God's Lioness and the Priest of Sycorax: Plath and Hughes," *Contemporary Literature*, 15 (Summer, 1974), 386–405. An exploration of Plath's and Hughes's psychological influence on each other as revealed in their similar poetic concerns, as a way of defining the individual vision of each.

MALOFF, SAUL. "The Poet as Cult Goddess," *Commonweal*, 103 (June 4, 1976), 371–74. A provocative bit of negative criticism. Maloff contends that the proliferating critical-biographical works on Plath create a myth which inflates the ordinary, but has little factual validity.

OATES, JOYCE CAROL. "The Death Throes of Romanticism: The Poems of Sylvia Plath," *Southern Review*, n.s.[9] (Summer, 1973), 501–22. An excellent and perceptive essay in which Oates, assuming Plath's significance as an artist and "as a cultural phenomenon," explores and defines both the individual and the cultural meaning of Plath's attitudes and dilemmas, as realized in her writing.

PERLOFF, MARJORIE G. "*Angst* and Animism in in the Poetry of Sylvia Plath," *Journal of Modern Literature*, 1 (1970), 57–74. An intelligent and well-documented essay, one of several published in 1970 to indicate growing critical attention to Plath as a major literary artist (also published in 1970: *The Art of Sylvia Plath*). Perloff explores Plath's poetry, especially the late work, in light of its paradoxical concern with animate and inanimate materials.

———. "On the Road to Ariel: The 'Transitional' Poetry of Sylvia Plath," *Iowa Review*, 4 (Spring, 1973), 94–110. An examination of ways in which Plath's so-called "transitional" poems are thematically similar but structurally inferior to the late poems. Perloff suggests that the perspective afforded by publication of the transitional volume diminishes the impresiveness of *Ariel*.

PHILLIPS, ROBERT. "The Dark Funnel: A Reading of Sylvia Plath," *Modern Poetry Studies*, 3 (Autumn, 1972), 49–74. Phillips explores his theory that the imagery of destruction in Plath's poems and novel results from the poet's reaction to her father's death, which Phillips calls the 'central myth" of her imagination.

ROSENSTEIN, HARRIET. "Reconsidering Sylvia Plath," *Ms.*, September 1972, pp. 44–51, 96–99. Asserting that Plath has been "falsely assigned" her "role as feminist heroine," Rosenstein examines the attitudes and temperaments of Plath's women.

SCHOLES, ROBERT. *"The Bell Jar,"* New York Times Book Review, April 11, 1971, p. 7. This excellent review of *The Bell Jar* on the occasion of its first American publication is astute, thought-provoking, and most enjoyable to read.

SMITH, STAN. "Attitudes Counterfeiting Life: The Irony of Artifice in Sylvia Plath's *The Bell Jar*," *Critical Quarterly*, 17 (Autumn, 1975), 247–60. An elaboration of Smith's view that *The Bell Jar*, not merely a psychological case history, is a "highly and originally structured novel."

THWAITE, ANTHONY. " 'I have never been so happy in my life': On Sylvia Plath," *Encounter*, 46 (June, 1976), 64–67. Review of *Letters Home*.

VENDLER, HELEN. *"Crossing the Water,"* New York Times Book Review, October 10, 1971, pp. 4, 48. This review of *Crossing the Water* one of the most enlightening of Plath's transitional poems. Vendler analyzes the unique qualities of the work of this period.

Index

(The works of Plath are listed under her name)

129